# VAN WOLVERTON'S GUIDE TO
# WINDOWS 3.1

## VAN WOLVERTON & MICHAEL BOOM

**RANDOM HOUSE**
**ELECTRONIC PUBLISHING**

New York

Van Wolverton's Guide to Windows 3.1

Copyright © 1992 by Van Wolverton and Michael Boom

Published in the United States by Random House, Inc., New York, and simultaneously in Canada by Random House of Canada, Ltd.

Manufactured in the United States of America

98765432   24689753   23456789

First edition

Library of Congress Cataloging-in-Publication Data

Wolverton, Van, 1939-
    Van Wolverton's guide to Windows 3.1 / by Van Wolverton and
Michael Boom.
        p.      cm.
    Includes index.
    ISBN 0-679-73912-2 : $20.00
    1. Windows (Computer programs) 2. Microsoft Windows (Computer
program)   I. Boom, Michael.   II. Title.
    QA76.76.W56W65   1992
    005.4'3—dc20                                          92-2280
                                                            CIP

The authors and publisher have used their best efforts in preparing this book. However, the authors and publisher make no warranties of any kind, express or implied, with regard to the documentation or data contained in this book, and specifically disclaim without limitation, any implied warranties of merchantability and fitness for a particular purpose with respect to the data contained therein, program listings in the book and/or the techniques described in the book. In no event shall the author or publisher be responsible or liable for any loss of profit or any other commercial damages, including but not limited to special, incidental, consequential or any other damages in connection with or arising out of furnishing, performance, or use of this book or the programs or data.

**Credits**
Art on pages 6, 17, 19, 26, and 43 by Sergei Goloshapov

**Trademarks**
A number of entered words in which we have reason to believe trademark, service mark, or other proprietary rights may exist have been designated as such by use of initial capitalization. However, no attempt has been made to designate as trademarks or service marks all personal computer words or terms in which proprietary rights might exist. The inclusion, exclusion or definition of a word or term is not intended to affect, or to express any judgment on, the validity or legal status of any proprietary right which may be claimed in that word or term.

*To my wife, Lynn, for keeping a window open for me.*

—MB

# ACKNOWLEDGMENTS

Writing any book is always a group endeavor, and I'm tickled pink to be working with Van Wolverton and the group at Random House Electronic Publishing on this one. My thanks to Van for including me in his series, working with my chapters as they trickled in, and loaning me vital equipment for writing. Thanks also to Claudette Moore, who brought the two of us together.

Publishing thanks go to Jane Mellin, tenacious project editor and facilitator; and to Michael Mellin for a delicious meal and inspiring conversation when I needed it most—midway through the book. For their clean book design and the chance to be caught in a limousine jam when I visited their Los Angeles office, thanks to Carol Barth and Greg Reynolds of Modern Design. (No, I was *not* in one of the limousines.) And for a last-minute emergency equipment loan, to work on toxic screen dumps, thanks to Mitchell Gass, who I hope has more time for bicycle riding and mushroom hunting in the future.

# CONTENTS

# Part III—Managing Your Computer System

# PREFACE

We react to computers in so many different ways. For millions, computers have become indispensable in the day-to-day operations of business, a mind-amplifying and labor-saving tool that arrived just in the nick of time. But that's by no means the only opinion. For some, computers are too complicated, too mysterious to contemplate. For others, computers are a threat, yet another manifestation of relentless technology that dehumanizes us all. For many—primarily those who came of age after the proliferation of personal computers—computers are no big deal, just another appliance like the TV or microwave.

I've yet to lose my sense of wonder at these remarkable machines. From my boyhood through middle age, I've watched computers move from the pages of science fiction stories to offices, schools, and homes everywhere. The computer that sits on my desk, the one I'm using to write this preface, has more computing power, more memory, and more disk storage than the first computer I laid hands on almost 30 years ago—and that computer was the only one on the campus of Colorado State University. I still find those facts remarkable.

If you're a writer, your opinion of computers influences how you write about them, adding to the challenges that face writers who collaborate. On the face of it, Michael Boom and I seem an unlikely pair. He's a baby boomer who lives in Oakland, CA, across the bay from the Silicon Valley; in a former life he was a concert oboist, and his wife is a ballet dancer. He's something of an expert on computer music and graphics. I'm too old to be a boomer—by some accounts, in fact, our oldest son just qualifies as one. I live in a log house on a ranch in Montana, seven miles from a town of 300; in a former life I was a newspaper reporter and technical writer. I'm something of a generalist: My computer knowledge is a lot like the Powder River, a mile wide and an inch deep.

Ah, but look closer. Michael Boom was raised in Livingston, Montana. I lived in Scotts Valley, California (the southern terminus of Silicon Valley) for thirteen years, where I worked for IBM and Intel and did freelance writing for several other computer companies. We both appreciate the fact that computers allow us to earn our keep doing something we enjoy. We both understand that people who don't know much about computers are otherwise quite intelligent, that people who want to learn to use a computer most likely aren't interested in becoming programmers or computer engineers, that writing a book about computers requires the same sort of concern for language and structure that any other good writing demands.

It's been a delight to work with Mike; I think the book reflects the success of the collaboration, and I hope you think so, too.

*Van Wolverton*
*Rubicon*
*Alberton, Montana*
*April 1992*

# INTRODUCTION

If Windows 3.1 is supposed to make your computer so much easier to use, then why are you thumbing through this book to learn how to use it? Because no matter how much you know about computers, using Windows for the first time requires some explanation. And although it all seems simple after you've used Windows awhile, the first few sessions can be frustrating.

That's why this book takes you through Windows step by step. In simple and clear words, it shows you Windows' main features and explains why they work the way they do. Tutorials sprinkled throughout the chapters show you how the features work in practice and teach your hands to do what your eyes read about. You'll also find occasional side comments that explain odd events that occur from time to time in Windows.

One thing this book does *not* do is try to explain everything there is to know about Windows. It concentrates instead on showing you the simplest and most direct ways to accomplish your work in Windows. When there are many alternative ways to accomplish the same task, this book narrows them down to give you only the easiest and most useful.

## Book Organization

This book is a trio of trios: Three sections of three chapters apiece. Read the first part to first get started with Windows; you'll see how to run Windows and start a program so you can get to work. Read the second section to feel comfortable with the programs you run in Windows; you'll find out how to use the features common to all Windows programs. And read the last part to see how Windows can help you manage your computer system; you'll see how to manage files on a disk, manage print jobs sent to a printer, and manage Windows itself to customize it to your taste.

If you have yet to install Windows on your computer, Appendix A gives you instructions to help you with installation. And to help you remember how to accomplish specific tasks in Windows, Appendix B lists the most common Windows tasks, with quick steps to accomplish each task—including keyboard steps if you work on a laptop computer without a mouse.

## What You Need to Read This Book

You'll need some free time and a computer that runs Windows version 3.1. This book assumes no previous knowledge of Windows, MS-DOS, or any other computer operating system. You do have to know how to turn your computer system on, but we'll take it from there.

It will help if your computer has a mouse or similar pointing device (such as a trackball), because Windows was designed to work with a pointer. To keep things simple, the steps and explanations in this book assume that you have a mouse. If you don't (laptop users often don't), you can find the keyboard equivalents for major Windows tasks in Appendix B.

If you have everything ready, then sit down, relax, and start in.

# PART I

## GETTING TO KNOW WINDOWS

Part I introduces you to the fundamentals of Windows: what Windows is and what it does; how you run Windows; and how files and directories are important for any program running in Windows. By the end of these three chapters, you should feel comfortable finding and starting a program in Windows. You should also know enough Windows basics to confidently explore on your own.

# CHAPTER
# 1

---

# WINDOWS AT WORK

Most tools have obvious functions. When you pick up a hammer, you know that you can use it to pound nails. When you turn on a blender, you know that you can frappé the living daylights out of unwitting fruits and vegetables. But when you sit down at a computer to use Windows, what kind of tool are you looking at, and what does it do for you? Some careful observation of Windows at work will show you.

## Life without Windows

To best understand the nature of Windows, consider first how your IBM-compatible computer works without Windows. When you flip the switch to turn it on, you hear the computer hum as it starts and then a slight chatter as it reads information from its fixed disk. What you hear is the computer's *hardware*—any part of the computer system that you can see, hear, or touch.

The computer's *software* is the intangible information the computer reads from the fixed disk. Like the information recorded in the grooves of a record or the microscopic pits of a CD, you can't see, hear, touch, smell, or taste the software—but you can sense its results. When software runs, it tells the hardware what to do: to display text and pictures on the monitor, to sort a list of names alphabetically, or to play music on an attached synthesizer.

### MS-DOS

Each piece of software your computer runs is called a *program*. And the first program your computer starts when you turn it on is MS-DOS (short for Microsoft Disk Operating System, also known simply as DOS). DOS controls the computer system at its most basic level. It senses the keys you press on the keyboard, it draws each character of text on the monitor, it stores information on disks and in memory, and it retrieves stored information. Your computer *must* run DOS in order to work or to run any other programs.

DOS acts much like the chief controller of a busy railroad yard. Just as the controller sets trains running and routes cargo from destination to destination, avoiding collisions, DOS starts programs and routes information from location to location in the computer's memory and on its disks. DOS remembers the location of each parcel of information so it can retrieve the information later. It also listens to requests from customers and follows them—if it understands them.

DOS's most important customer is you. Typically, when you work at a computer without Windows, you talk to DOS by typing in commands at the keyboard. DOS follows those commands, moving information from place to place, performing calculations and any other necessary work, and then displays messages in text on the monitor to let you know the results of your command.

Because your communication with DOS is limited to text, you and DOS must both describe your requests and actions in precise words. If you don't know exactly which word to use for a command and what information you must include with the word, DOS, exacting bureaucrat that it is, will shrug its invisible shoulders and do nothing. And don't even think of mispelling commands.

## Application Programs

DOS has other customers as well as you: it also serves *application programs* (or simply *applications*) as shown in Figure 1-1. You typically buy applications from a software dealer; they range from simple mailing label programs to complex page layout programs and spreadsheets. When you run applications, they concentrate on specific tasks to serve you, tasks such as checking spelling, organizing a data base, or calculating values in a spreadsheet. They call on DOS whenever they need system work performed. For example, they might ask DOS to save figures to disk, to send a letter out to the printer for printing, or to retrieve names in a mailing list stored earlier.

An application running on your computer communicates directly with DOS; it also communicates directly with you through its own display on the monitor. It expects you to tell it what to do, using commands that it understands. Because the companies that write application programs each have their own philosophies about program design, the commands you use in one application can differ substantially from those you use in another application, even if the job you want to perform is the same. For example, one word processor may require you to give it a "load" command to retrieve a letter stored on a disk; another may require "open"; and a third may require you to hold down the F3 and Shift keys while typing the first letter of the second verse of the "Star Spangled Banner."

*Figure 1-1* DOS controls the computer system and serves you and any running application programs. Applications communicate directly with DOS and with you.

So—in a world without Windows, you spend a lot of time memorizing commands and learning new ways to work with each application you buy.

# Enter Windows

Like DOS, Windows is *system software*: it handles basic computer system tasks. It doesn't replace DOS, however, but works in partnership with it—something like a sympathetic station agent who shows you actions you can take, accepts your choice, and then goes into the back office to tell the chief controller how to accomplish what you just asked for. By standing in between you and DOS, Windows acts as an intermediary who is much easier to communicate with than DOS.

## Windows Provides a Visual Work Environment

One of the reasons Windows is easier to use than DOS is that it isn't limited to text alone for communication. It mixes pictures and words on the screen to give you a vivid, easy-to-grasp image of the actions you're taking. To help you work in a familiar environment, Windows creates a desktop on your screen and lays out work areas on top of it as you would lay out sheets of paper on a real desktop (as shown in Figure 1-2). Windows also provides symbols on the desktop that represent actions or packets of information, and it lets you point at symbols using a pointing device such as a mouse, a touch screen, or a pen and tablet.

Windows does offer text commands, but it doesn't require that you memorize each command along with its exact spelling and usage. When you want to issue a command, Windows opens a *menu*—a list of commands you can make. You point to the command you want, and Windows prompts you for any additional information it needs to carry out the command.

## Windows Provides a Standard Work Environment

Windows also acts as an intermediary for application programs. By standing between you and an application, Windows provides the same visual representation for application activities that it does for

DOS activities. And because any application communicating with you through Windows must conform to Windows' methods of working, you perform common activities the same way in every application. Saving a letter in a word processor works the same way as saving a report in a spreadsheet program; printing a letter works the same way as printing a report.

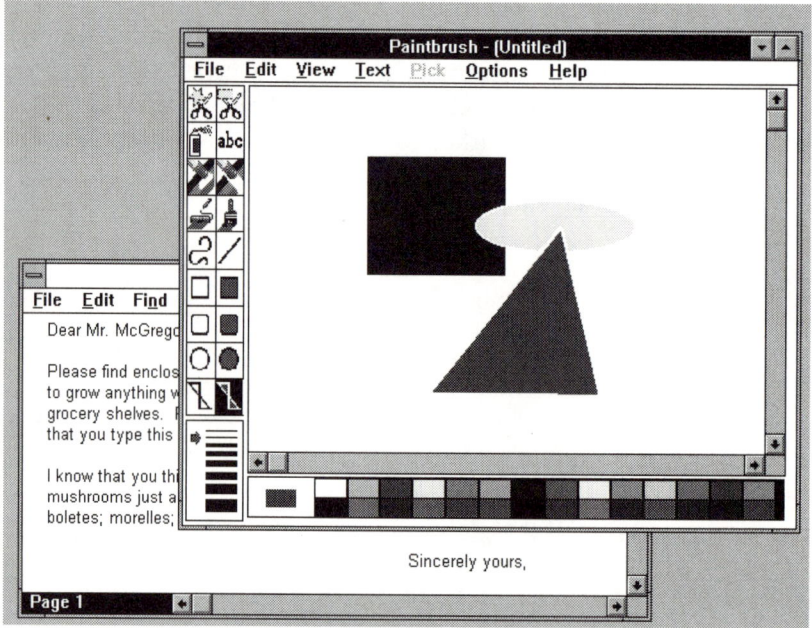

*Figure 1-2* Windows turns the monitor screen into a desktop with separate areas laid out here for a word processor and a paint program.

By imposing standards on the way applications work, Windows creates a standard work environment, where you don't have to learn an entirely new way of working for each application you use. The fundamentals are the same from program to program. With a little exploration, you can often learn the basics of a new application running under Windows without reading a manual. And if you can't find the manual when you're stumped, Windows provides a manual built into the software. You ask Windows for help on a specific topic; Windows presents text on the screen explaining the topic, as shown in Figure 1-3.

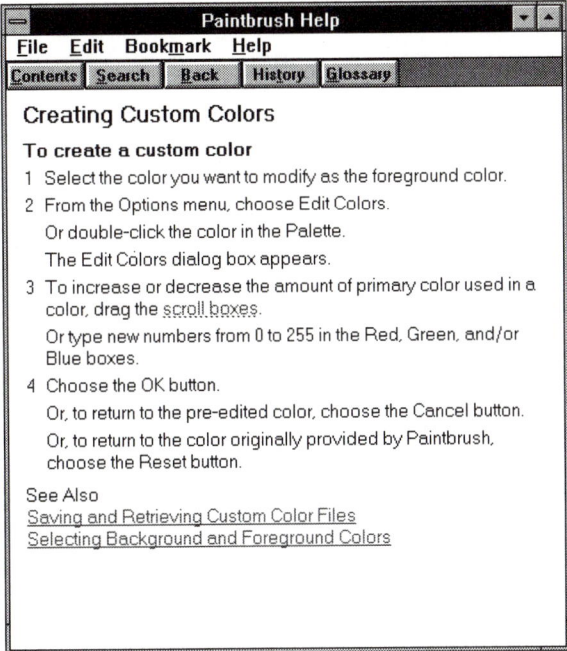

*Figure 1-3* Windows can give you information about a program's features.

## Windows Provides a Custom Work Environment

Although Windows imposes standards on the applications that work with it, it doesn't impose standards on you. You can tailor Windows to look and act the way that works best for you, much as you organize the desk in your office or home to match your working style. Windows provides controls that set—among other things—the colors and patterns you see on the screen, the types of characters used to present text, the way the keyboard and the mouse respond to you, and the sound you hear as an alert.

## Windows Provides Tools for Managing Your Computer System

Windows is more than system software that creates a visual workplace for your work; it's also a set of programs that you can run to manage your computer system. These programs, an integral part of Windows, perform many of the common jobs you'd otherwise have to do using DOS. They check the contents of disks, duplicate and erase information, start application programs, copy information to a floppy disk, set up an attached printer so that it prints correctly, and take care of other daily computer tasks—all using the simple visual work techniques you use in any program running with Windows.

### So What Comes with Windows, Anyway?

Microsoft (Windows' publisher) ships Windows in a snappy box filled with floppy disks, an accompanying manual, and miscellaneous advertising flyers. One of the floppy disks contains a program called Win Setup which, when you run it, copies Windows and all of its attendant programs from the floppy disks onto the fixed disk in your computer (a process you can read more about in Appendix A, if you're interested). So what do you end up with after Windows is installed? You get its main programs, which are:

- **Program Manager** To start application programs

- **File Manager** To move information from place to place on a disk or between disks, or to look at the contents of a disk

- **Print Manager** To feed information from application programs to the printer attached to your system

- **Control Panel** To customize the Windows environment so it looks and acts the way you want it to

- **Clipboard** To transfer information from one application to another application

You also get three main application programs, which are:

- **Write** For writing letters and other documents
- **Paintbrush** For creating color drawings

*(continued)*

*So What Comes with Windows, Anyway? (continued)*

- **Terminal** For sending information back and forth over the phone lines to other computers

   Windows also provides eleven smaller applications for specific uses such as logging appointments and keeping addresses.

Besides these system management programs, Windows also includes a set of its own simple application programs. These applications let you draw colorful pictures, write letters, connect your computer over the phone to other computers, keep track of appointments and addresses, and perform other useful jobs. They're not as powerful as most applications you can buy—you'll find it hard to use them to lay out a newsletter or to juggle a data base of thousands of addresses, for example—but they often do the trick. And the price is right.

**Windows Modes**

All computers are not created equal. Some are more powerful than others; they run faster and they can store information in their memory more efficiently. Windows is designed to run on standard IBM-compatible computers and, at the same time, to take advantage of features on more powerful computers. To do this, Windows can operate in either one of two separate ways. Each different way of operating is called a *mode*. The first—*Standard mode*—works on standard computers. The second—*Enhanced mode*—runs on computers with the powerful 80386 or 80486 central processors. (A central processor is the heart of the computer and gives it much of its capabilities.)

*(continued)*

*Windows Modes (continued)*

When the Win Setup program installs Windows on a computer system, it evaluates the type of computer and its capabilities, and then sets Windows to run in the appropriate mode. This book describes Windows as it runs in Standard mode. If you're fortunate enough to work with Windows on a system that can run Enhanced mode, you may find some slight differences from the descriptions here, but nothing to lose sleep over. They're all—as the name implies—enhancements that make Windows work even more efficiently.

You've now seen what Windows can do when it's at work, and should have a much better idea of what kind of tool it is. In the next chapter, you get your hands on Windows—or at least as close as your hand can come to a piece of intangible software.

# CHAPTER
# 2

---

# EXPLORING WINDOWS

The best way to learn Windows is to try it—start it, poke it to see if it's alive, and play with it for a while. As you explore Windows with the hands-on examples in this chapter, you get a feel for the way Windows works and how it can work for you. When you're done, you'll know how to start a program in Windows and how to choose commands from the program's menus.

## Starting Up

The first step for any Windows session is to start your computer and Windows. Try it now:

1. Switch on your computer and monitor and then sit back to wait for MS-DOS to load and start. (It should do so automatically.)

   After a brief wait, you'll see text appear on the screen with details about how MS-DOS is running. You can ignore the text.

2. Wait for MS-DOS to ask you for a command. It asks with a *prompt*, which is this line:

   ```
   C>_
   ```

   The underline blinks on and off to let you know that MS-DOS is ready for you to type. (The prompt on your computer may use a D, E, or other letter instead of a C in the prompt, but don't worry about it. MS-DOS works the same regardless of the letter in the prompt.)

3. Type three letters after the prompt: win. When you're finished, press the Enter key.

   This is how you enter a command in MS-DOS: You type the letters of the command and then press the Enter key to tell your computer you've finished typing. The command in this case is Win, which tells MS-DOS that you want it to run Windows.

   After you've entered the Win command, Windows displays a colorful startup picture and then proceeds to load itself from disk and start running. After a short interval, the startup picture disappears and is replaced by the Windows *desktop* as shown in Figure 2-1.

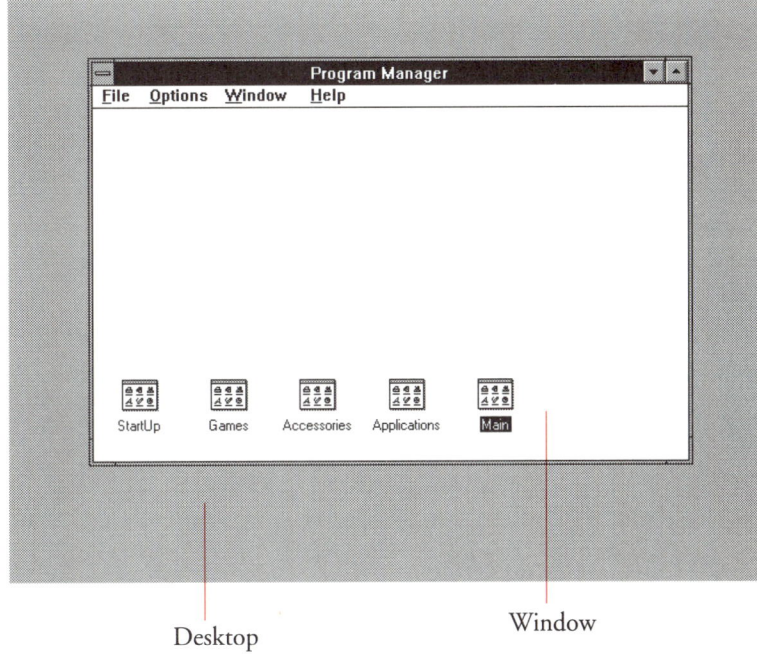

Figure 2-1 When you run Windows, it presents you with its desktop and a window lying on top of it.

### I Can't Start Windows!

You just turned on your computer, started MS-DOS, and entered the Win command when you saw the prompt. But MS-DOS came back with the retort, *Bad command or file name* instead of starting Windows. What's wrong?

Chances are that Windows isn't installed on your computer or it isn't installed properly. You have to install (or reinstall) Windows. The easiest way, of course, is to ask someone else to do it. That's what your computer dealer or your company's system administrator is for. But if you'd like to install Windows on your own, it's not too hard, and you'll find instructions in Appendix A at the back of this book.

## The Desktop and a Window

Windows' desktop is, in appearance, simply a muted backdrop. However, like a real desktop, Windows' desktop is not remarkable for itself but for what lies upon it. And what lies on top of Windows' desktop now is a window, the most important element of Windows, and the reason for Windows' name.

A window is a discrete work area on the desktop. Windows creates a separate window for each running program to provide a place on the desktop for the program to work. When the program displays information, it does so only within the boundaries of its window. When you give commands to the program, you do so by using controls and menus located within the window.

When you run more than one program at a time, windows may overlap. In fact, one window may completely cover another, just as pieces of paper on a real desktop cover each other. Using a mouse and pointer, however, you can drag a window from one location to another, set one window on top of another, or retrieve a covered window from beneath other windows.

The window you see when you first run Windows is the Program Manager window. It belongs to Program Manager, an application program whose job is starting other programs. Program Manager is inextricably linked with Windows. When you run Windows, you automatically run Program Manager. And when you quit Program Manager, you quit Windows.

# Rummaging around the Desktop

When you work on a real desktop, you move paper and books around with your hands, and you write with a pen or pencil. When you work with Windows' desktop, you move windows around with a mouse and pointer, and you write text with a keyboard. Although a keyboard is familiar to most computer users, a mouse is a new experience for some. Try it to see how it works:

1. Rest your normal writing hand (left or right) on the mouse with your index finger on one mouse button and the second finger on the next mouse button as shown in Figure 2-2.

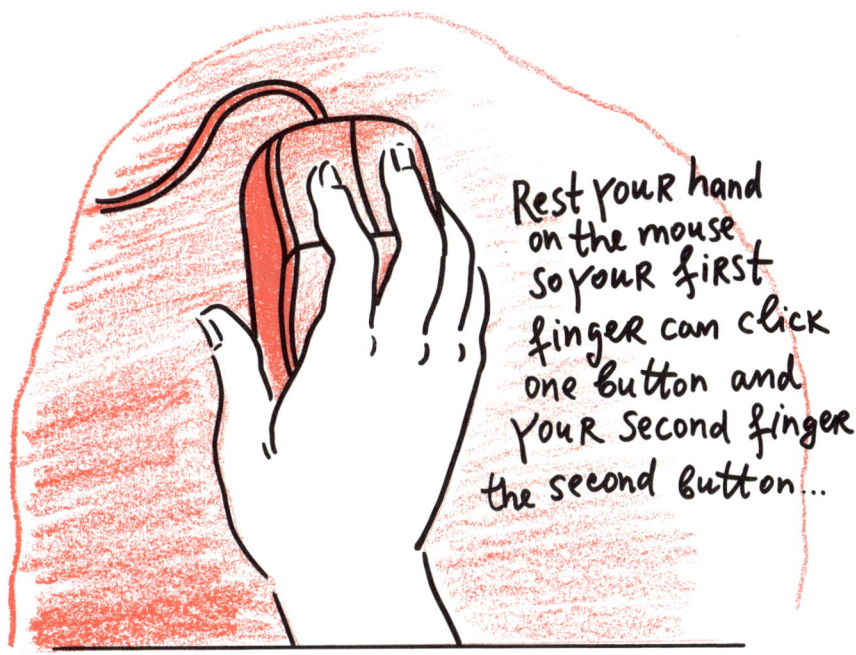

*Rest your hand on the mouse so your first finger can click one button and your second finger the second button...*

*Figure 2-2* Rest your hand on the mouse so your first finger can click one button and your second finger the second button.

2. Roll the mouse on a flat area next to your keyboard. As you roll, notice the small, moving arrow on your monitor.

   The moving arrow is the *pointer*. It responds to the direction you roll the mouse. As you roll forward, the pointer moves up. As you roll back, the pointer moves down. And as you roll left or right, the pointer moves left or right.

3. Roll the mouse so the pointer moves to each of the four corners of the screen.

   You may run out of space for the mouse as you roll in one direction. If so, pick up the mouse as shown in Figure 2-3, carry it in the opposite direction, put it back down, and continue rolling as before. Rolling the small ball on the underside of the mouse moves the pointer; if you pick the mouse up, the ball doesn't roll, so you can move the mouse wherever you want without moving the pointer.

### Windows Doesn't Look the Same on My Computer

When you start Windows on your computer, it may look different than the figures in this chapter. Because Windows is a tool you can customize, it can take on different appearances at the request of its users, using different colors, text, and background patterns, for example. If you're working through this book at a computer that is shared with other people, someone else may have customized Windows for themselves. The pictures in this chapter show Windows as it runs after it has first been installed on a computer, so they might not match what you see in a customized version of Windows. Similarly, the colors described here are the colors Windows uses when it is first started up. Don't worry about the visual differences—they're superficial and won't affect the way Windows works.

You may also find that Windows on your computer starts with more than one window. This is probably because somebody else used Windows, opened up several windows, and then quit Windows. Windows can remember open windows from session to session if you ask it to, which lets you go back to Windows as you left it (the equivalent of leaving papers out on a real desktop).

To get rid of the extra windows (and to find the Program Manager window if it's not visible), try this:

1. Move the pointer so that its tip touches the small box in the upper-left corner of an extra window, then click the left mouse button. A menu appears with a list of commands from which you can choose.

2. Move the pointer so its tip touches the Close command, then click the left mouse button. Windows removes the window from the screen.

Repeat these steps for each cluttering window, until you see only the Program Manager window.

*Figure 2-3* Pick the mouse up and move it back a bit if you run out of room while rolling the mouse.

4. Move the pointer so that its tip touches the border of the window.

   Notice that the pointer changes shape to a two-headed arrow while on the border. Windows changes the pointer's shape whenever the pointer touches a place where you can take a special action. In this case, the pointer changes to a two-headed arrow because you can use it to move the border of the window.

Now that you can move the pointer around the desktop, the next step is to tell Windows that you're interested in something underneath the tip of the pointer. This is where the left mouse button comes into play:

1. Move the pointer so its tip touches one of the symbols in the Program Manager window as shown in Figure 2-4. (Each one of these symbols is called an *icon*.)

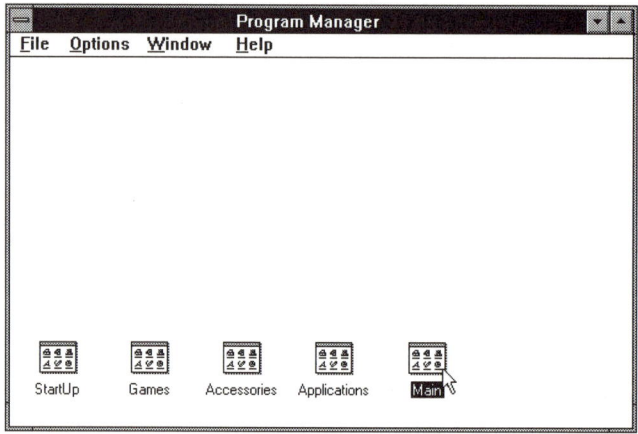

*Figure 2-4* The pointer rests on an icon. The icon is highlighted, which shows that it is selected.

2. Click the left mouse button: push down and let up quickly.

   This tells Windows you're interested in the icon under the pointer, a process called *selection*. Windows responds by opening a menu with commands that affect the icon. It also darkens the icon name, a technique Windows uses to make the selected item stand out on the screen. The darkening is called *highlighting*.

3. Move the pointer away from the icon, out of its menu, and onto an empty spot in the window or on the desktop. Then click the left mouse button.

The icon's menu closes and the icon is no longer highlighted. By clicking on an empty spot, you told Windows that you're no longer interested in the icon or its menu, so Windows returned the selected icon to its normal state. This is called *deselecting* an item because it's the opposite of selecting the item.

The mouse has two buttons, left and right, but you use only the left button for common Windows tasks. Whenever this book or a manual says "click," you can safely assume it means click the left mouse button. The right button is only used in rare circumstances within certain programs, but not at all for common Windows tasks.

# Working with a Window

Now that you can use the mouse and pointer to point and select, try working with a typical window: the Program Manager window. You can change its size, move it around, and tuck it conveniently out of the way when necessary.

1. Move the pointer to the Program Manager label, which is the blue strip at the top of the window. (This label—the text and its blue background—is called the *title bar*.)

2. Hold the left mouse button down and, as you hold, roll the mouse.

   An outline of the window moves with the pointer as you roll.

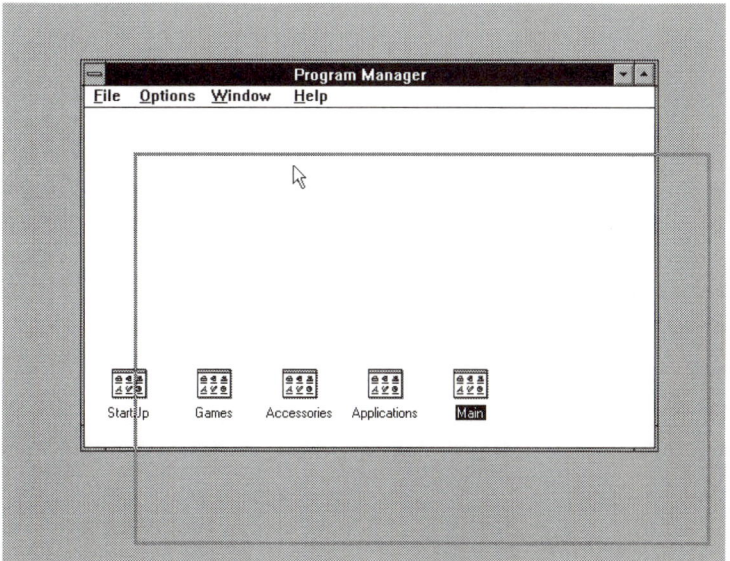

3. Release the left mouse button.

The window moves to the location of the window outline you set with the pointer.

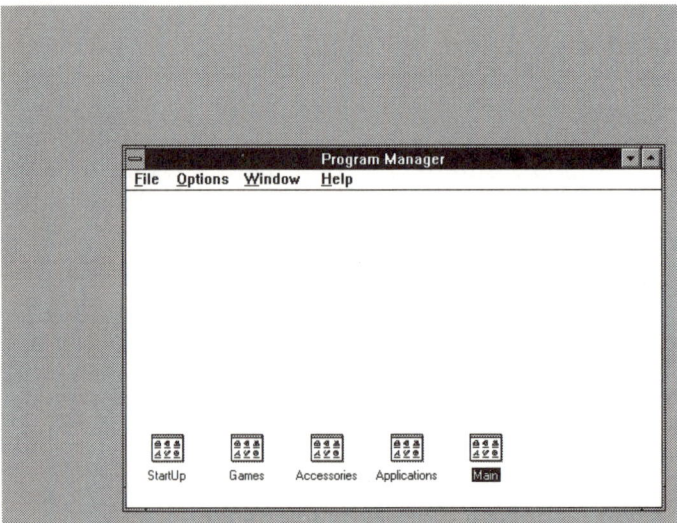

You just *dragged* the window from one location to another. To drag an object, you hold down the left mouse button while rolling the mouse. To drag a window, you must point to its title bar while dragging.

4. Move the pointer to any corner of the window so the pointer turns into a diagonally pointing two-headed arrow.

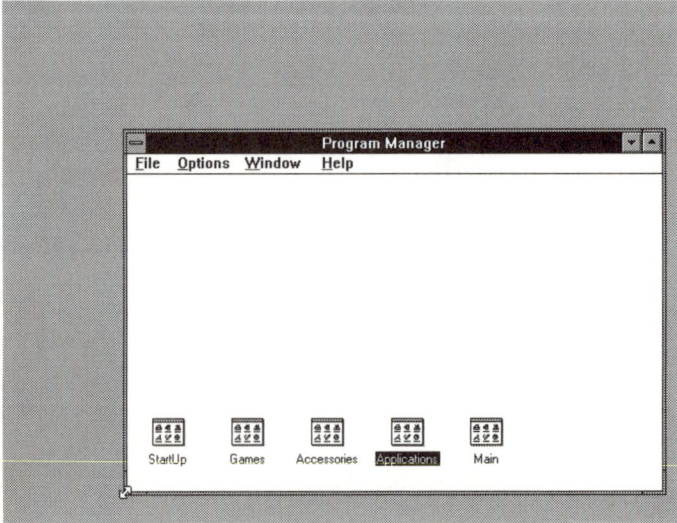

5. Drag the window's corner: hold down the left mouse button and roll the mouse.

   As you drag, the outline of the window moves with you, enlarging or reducing the size of the window as you move the corner in or out.

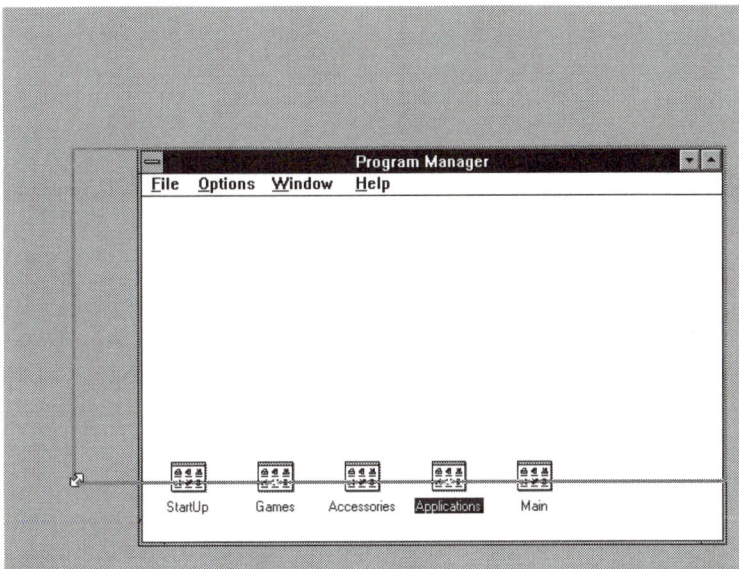

6. Release the mouse button.

   The window resizes itself to the new shape you set. You can drag any of the window's four sides or corners to resize it as you wish.

7. Drag a corner of the window inward so that the window is small—small enough not to be able to display all of the Program Manager's icons. When the window resizes, some of the icons are hidden. New controls appear along the right and bottom sides of the window as shown in Figure 2-5. These are *scroll bars*.

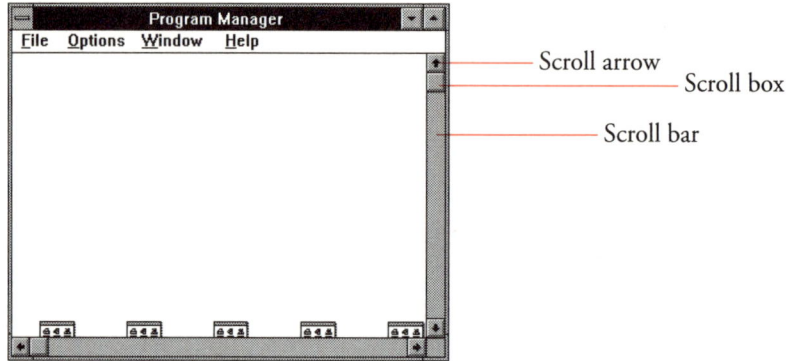

*Figure 2-5* Use scroll bars to reveal hidden parts of a window's interior.

## What Are the Parts of a Window?

So what are all those things in a window, anyway? It helps to know their names if you ask someone else for help or leaf through manuals for Windows applications. Figure 2-6 shows it all.

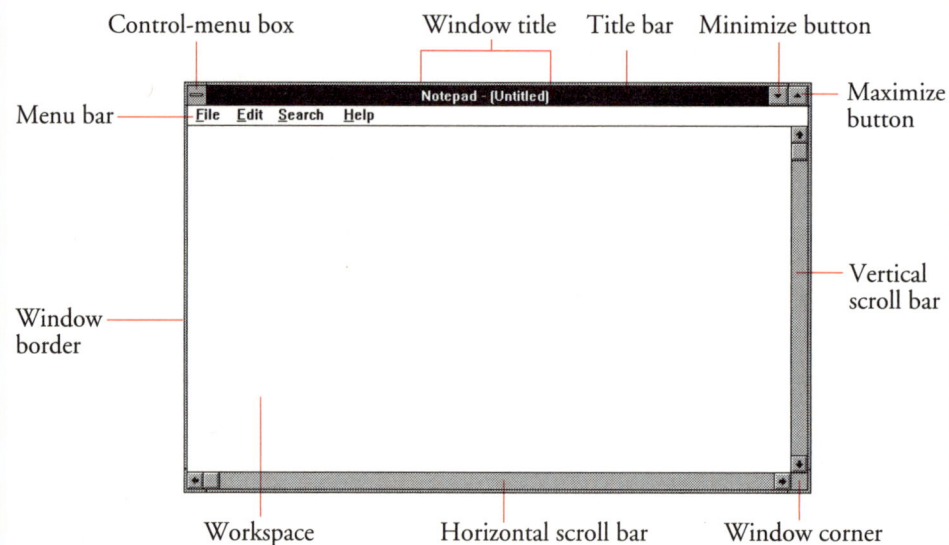

*Figure 2-6* The parts of a window each have a different function.

Not every window contains all of these parts. For example, some programs don't want you to resize the window, so they don't offer you a maximize box.

## Using Scroll Bars

When you resize a window, you can reduce it enough in size so that it covers some of the contents of the window's *workspace* (the interior of the window). When this happens, Windows doesn't cut the hidden contents from the window; it simply tucks them out of sight, beyond the window's boundaries. It then adds scroll bars to the sides of the windows so you can bring hidden workspace contents back into view.

To understand what scroll bars do, look at the drawing in Figure 2-7. The window's workspace is like a large map viewed through the window. You see only the part of the workspace that is inside the window's border; anything outside is invisible. A scroll bar slides (*scrolls*) the workspace in one direction or another to move hidden parts of the workspace into the interior of the window, where you can see it.

Windows adds scroll bars to a window only if the window's workspace contains items that are hidden beyond the window's borders. A horizontal scroll bar scrolls the workspace left and right, and a vertical scroll bar scrolls the workspace up and down. Windows determines in what directions the workspace must scroll to reveal hidden items and adds the appropriate scroll bars.

To use a scroll bar, drag the small white box within it (called the *scroll box*) along the length of the scroll bar. Try it now:

1. Move the tip of the pointer to the scroll box in the vertical scroll bar (the scroll bar that stretches up and down), then drag the scroll box up (or down, if up isn't available) and release it when you get to a new position.

   The interior of the window quickly scrolls up or down to a new location in the workspace, revealing previously hidden icons.

2. Drag the scroll box of the horizontal scroll bar to a new location and release it.

   The interior of the window scrolls left or right to a new workspace location, again revealing hidden icons.

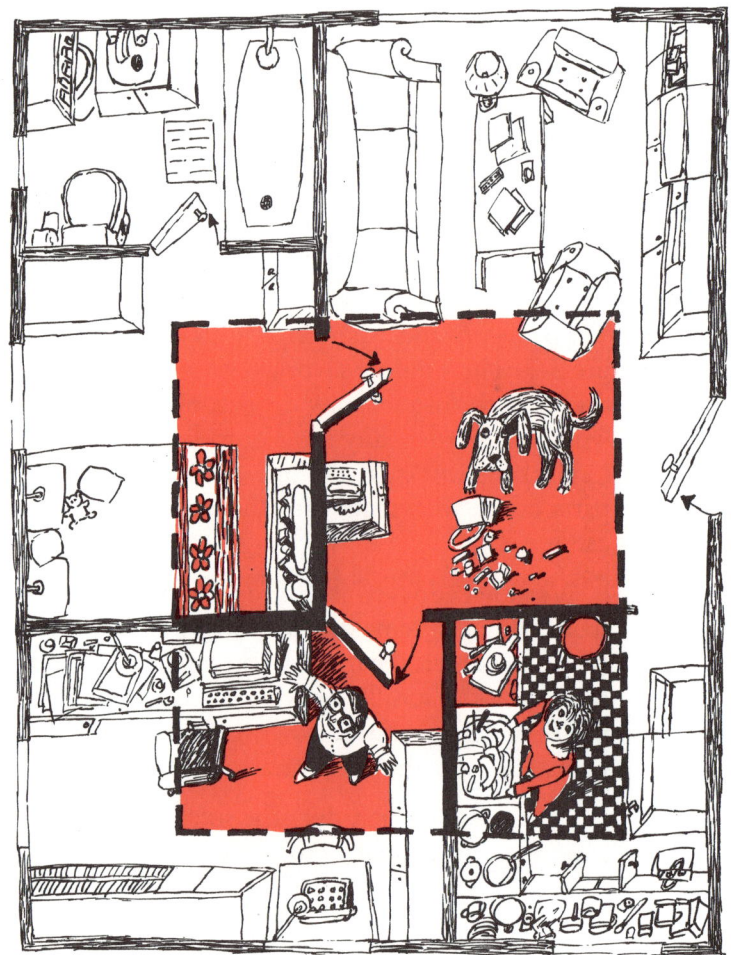

*Figure 2-7* The interior of a window looks at a part of the window's workspace. The window's scroll bars move the workspace under the window to reveal hidden sections of the workspace.

The position of the scroll box along a scroll bar tells you what section of the workspace you see in the windows. If the scroll box is in the middle of the scroll bar, you're looking at the middle of the workspace. If the scroll box is at one end of the scroll bar, you're looking at that end of the workspace.

## Quickly Resizing a Window

Windows offers two options for quickly resizing a window: the *maximize button,* which expands a window to fill the entire screen; and the *minimize button,* which tucks the window away as an icon to clear up the desktop. Both of these options let you resize windows without dragging their borders. Try them out on the Program Manager window:

1. Click on the maximize button—the button in the upper right corner of the window, labeled with an up arrow. (To click on the button, move the pointer tip onto it and click the left mouse button.)

   The Program Manager window grows to fill the entire screen, and the maximize button changes its label to show both an up and a down arrow.

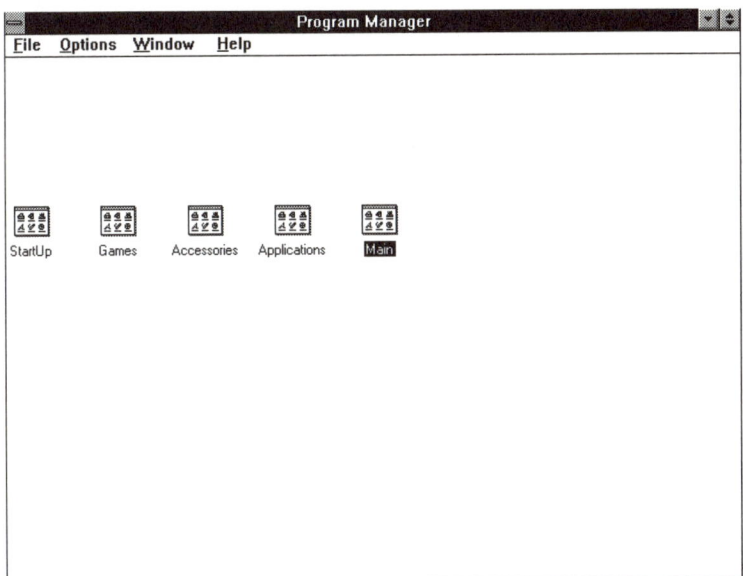

2. Click on the maximize button once again.

   The window returns to its original size and the maximize button is once again labeled with an up arrow.

3. Click on the minimize button, which is the button next to the maximize button. It's labeled with a down arrow.

The window disappears, and in its place is an icon labeled *Program Manager*, located in the lower left corner of the desktop.

4. To restore the icon to a window, *double-click* on the icon. To double-click an object in Windows, move the tip of the pointer onto it, then click the left mouse button twice rapidly.

The icon disappears, and the window reappears in its previous size and position.

When you run many different programs in Windows, the desktop can get cluttered with windows. Turning windows into icons is a convenient way to clear up the desktop without quitting programs. Whenever you need to use a minimized window, simply double-click on its icon to reopen it.

## Choosing Commands from a Menu

You can do most of your work on the desktop by clicking, double-clicking, and dragging with the mouse and pointer. Within a window, you can do additional work by choosing commands from menus.

To open a menu, click on a spot that has a menu attached. You did this once already when you clicked on an icon in the Program Manager. The menu attached to the icon popped open for you to read its contents.

To choose a command from an open menu, simply click on the command. Try it out:

1. Click on the *control-menu box* (a light gray box labeled with a bar) at the top left corner of the Program Manager.

   A menu pops open. This is the window's *control menu,* filled with commands that control the window.

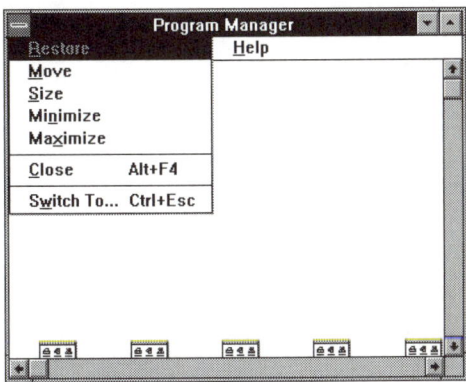

2. Click on the *Minimize* command in the menu.

   The menu closes after accepting your command, and the window is minimized: it turns into a window icon.

3. Click on the Program Manager icon.

   Its control menu pops open again.

4. Click on the *Restore* command in the menu.

   The menu closes and the icon is turned back into a window.

5. Find the *menu bar*—it's the horizontal white strip along the top of the window with the labels *File, Options, Window,* and, *Help.* Click on the label *File* to open the File menu.

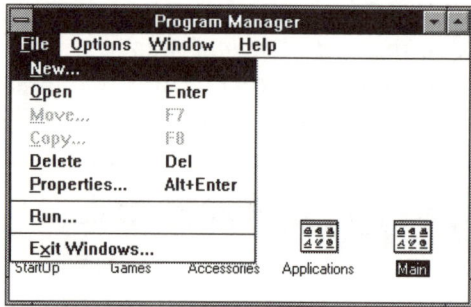

6. Click on the label *Options* in the menu bar.

   The File menu closes and the Options menu opens in its place.

7. Click on the *Help* label in the menu bar.

   The Options menu closes and the Help menu opens.

8. Click on the command *About Program Manager* in the Help menu.

   The menu closes and a box appears on the screen with information about Program Manager (what version is running, who the program is licensed to, and more).

9. Click on the OK button in the upper right corner of the box to close the box.

   Some helpful observations about using menus:

   • Every window (and program icon, when the window is minimized) has a control menu that controls the window. You don't often have to use the control menu if you have a mouse and pointer because you can accomplish the same tasks by clicking and dragging. The commands are there for Windows users who work from a keyboard alone.

   • The menu bar at the top of a window offers program menus with commands that control the window's program. Each of the menus is a logical group of commands with its own name; you see the menu names in the menu bar.

- When you click on a command, the menu closes and the command is carried out.
- Click anywhere outside of an open menu to close the menu without choosing a command.

### Using Windows without a Mouse

Running Windows without a mouse (or similar pointing device) is like trying to type using a toothpick in your mouth. You can do it, but it takes longer, and you might cut loose with a few choice swear words. A mouse isn't expensive, and it comes with many desktop systems, so there's no good reason to run Windows with a keyboard alone—unless you happen to be sitting on a crowded plane working on a laptop computer. If so, these techniques can help you work with windows and menus without a mouse:

- Press the Alt key and the space bar at the same time to open a window's control menu.
- Use the up and down arrow keys on your keyboard to highlight a command you want in the menu, then press Enter to choose the command and close the menu.
- If you choose a window control command that normally uses a pointer (like Move or Resize), you can use the arrow keys to move a window or border outline to the position you want. Press Enter when you get the position you want, and the window will resize or move to the outline position.
- Once you've opened the control menu, you can open the menus in the menu bar by pressing the left or right arrow keys. You can choose commands from any of these menus just as you do in the control menu.

For specific instructions on accomplishing standard Windows tasks with a keyboard alone, take a look at Appendix B at the back of the book.

## Starting a Program

Now it's time to start a program using Program Manager. Try starting Notepad, a simple application included with Windows:

1. Drag one of the Program Manager's window corners out until
   you can see all the icons within the window.

2. Move the pointer onto the icon in the Program Manager window labeled *Accessories* and double-click on the icon.

   The icon opens into a window labeled *Accessories* that contains
   a collection of programs. Each of the icons you see in this window represents a program that you can start.

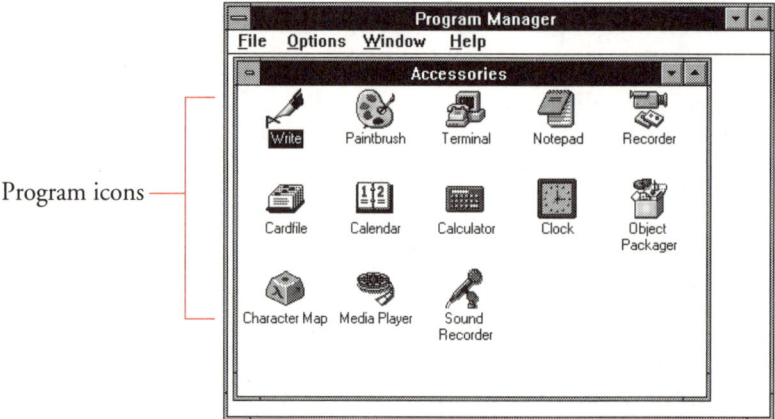

3. Double-click the icon labeled *Notepad.*

   This starts Notepad, an application designed for writing
   simple documents. Notepad appears on the screen in its own
   window, labeled *Notepad - (Untitled)*, which lays on top of the
   Program Manager window. Notice that the Notepad window
   has its own set of menus in the menu bar. These menus contain commands that work specifically for Notepad.

4. If the Notepad window completely covers the Program Manager window, drag the Notepad window by its title bar (the
   blue strip at the top) until you can see part of the Program
   Manager window.

5. Click on any part of the Program Manager window.

The Program Manager window and its Accessories window pop out on top of the Notepad window.

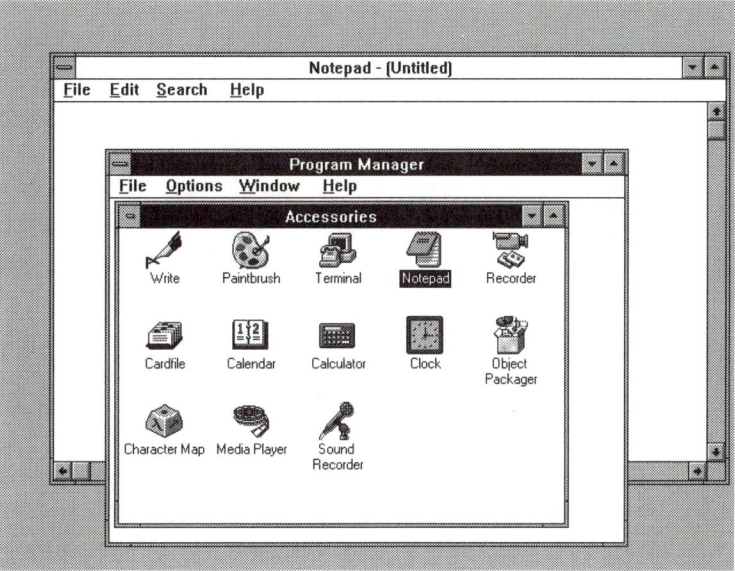

6. Click on any part of the Notepad window.

The Notepad window pops out on top of the other windows.

7. Click on the *File* menu name in the menu bar of the Notepad window to open the File menu.

8. Click on the command *Exit.*

Notepad quits, and the Notepad window closes.

9. Move the pointer to the control-menu box in the upper left corner of the Accessories window and double-click.

The Accessories window closes. Double-clicking a window's control-menu box is one more method—a quick one—for closing a window.

You've now started and quit a program in Windows. You'll find many different programs available in Program Manager, all stored in different collections of programs such as Accessories and Main.

These collections are called *program groups*. You can start any one of the programs by first opening the program group to which it belongs and then double-clicking on its icon. To quit a program once you've started it, choose *Exit* from its File menu.

When you have more than one application running (as you did with Program Manager and Notepad), their windows may overlap. To bring a window to the top, all you need to do is click in the window. The top window is called the *active window* because that's the one where you're working; Windows marks the active window by coloring its title bar blue. All other windows have a white title bar.

## Shutting Down

When you're finished working with Windows, you shut down by first quitting Windows and then turning off your computer. When you quit, Windows takes a few moments to save information to disk. It uses that information when you start Windows again later. If you shut the computer off without quitting Windows or, worse yet, shut the computer off while Windows is in the process of saving information to disk, then Windows may have trouble starting up properly for the next session. This is how you should shut down at the end of a Windows session:

1.  Click on *File* in Program Manager's menu bar to open the File menu.

2.  Click on the command *Exit Windows* in the File menu to quit Program Manager and Windows together.

    Windows presents a box with a message to make sure you really want to quit. The box says, *This will end your Windows session*, and offers you two choices: *OK* and *Cancel.*

3.  Click on *OK* to exit Windows.

    The screen goes blank, and after a few seconds you're back to the MS-DOS prompt (*C>* or a variation) where you started Windows. Windows has now completely quit and has saved any information it must save to disk.

4.  Turn off your computer and your monitor.

You're finished with your Windows exploration, unless you want to go off on your own for a while. You know how to start and quit Windows, and how to handle Windows basics while you run Windows: how to use the pointer to point and select, how to move and resize windows, how to choose commands from menus, and how to start and quit programs. The next chapter introduces you to the concept of a file and shows you how to find your way around the contents of a disk.

# CHAPTER
# 3

---

# EXPLORING FILES

When you work at a desk, you shuffle papers. When you work at a computer, you shuffle files—the digital equivalent of papers. Files are so essential to any kind of work you do with Windows that this chapter is devoted to files—what they are, how they're organized, and how you can look at the way they're stored on a disk. Once you understand how Windows handles files, you'll find that everyday Windows operations make much more sense.

## What Is a File?

Put simply, a file is stored information. It's usually stored on a hard disk or a floppy disk, and is always given a name so that you can ask for the file later by name. When you write a letter in a word processor and save the letter to disk, you save the letter in a file. When you create a data base containing a mailing list, you save the list in a file. And when you buy a program that comes on a floppy disk, that program is stored in a file—or perhaps in several files that work together.

You save information in files because a computer's memory is fleeting. Once you switch the computer off, everything in its memory disappears in a flash of electrons. Any work you had in the computer's memory won't be there when you turn the computer back on. Work stored on a disk, however, doesn't go away when the power goes off because information is encoded magnetically on the disk's surface (much like music is recorded on cassette tape). When you turn the computer back on, it can read stored information from disk files and put the information into computer memory where you can continue your work.

Files on disk also extend the capacity of your computer. A typical hard disk can easily store ten, twenty, or even 50 times more information than the computer's memory can. If you're working with a large amount of information—such as a mailing list with hundreds of thousands of names or the manuscript of a full book—the computer keeps the information in a disk file and reads only as much of it as it needs to work with at one time. When it finishes with the information it read, it can clear the information from its memory and read in more information from the disk file.

Because you and your computer constantly work with files on disk and because those files stay there even after you switch off the power, a disk eventually gets cluttered with files, which makes it difficult to find what you need or—if the disk gets too full—to store new files. To help with your housecleaning (or disk cleaning, as the case may be), Windows offers File Manager.

# File Manager

File Manager, as its name implies, manages files stored on a disk or a similar storage device. It's one of Windows' main application programs, and is designed to help you put your digital finger on precisely the file you want, or to sweep away briskly the files you don't want. You can use File Manager to prepare disks for file storage, to organize files on a disk so they're easy to find, to copy or rename files, to print out the contents of files, to search for a specific file, or to perform many other file-related tasks.

You start File Manager just as you do other Windows applications: you use Program Manager. Try it now with the following steps:

1. Turn on your computer now, if it's not on already, and run Windows.

2. Double-click on the icon labeled *Main* in the Program Manager window.

   A window named *Main* opens, showing the contents of the Main program group.

3. Double-click on the icon labeled *File Manager* (which is appropriately shaped like a filing cabinet).

   File Manager starts and presents its window.

4. Click on the File Manager window's maximize button (in the upper right corner of the window).

   The window expands to fill the entire screen, which allows File Manager to display as much information at one time as possible. It should look something like Figure 3-1.

Notice that File Manager has a window within a window. The inner window, along with other inner windows which you can open in File Manager, allows you to divide the workspace of the File Manager window into separate work areas for File Manager business. You'll learn how to do this in Chapter 7. For now, follow the next step to expand the inner window so that it fills the outer window and merges with it.

Inner window's maximize button

Inner window

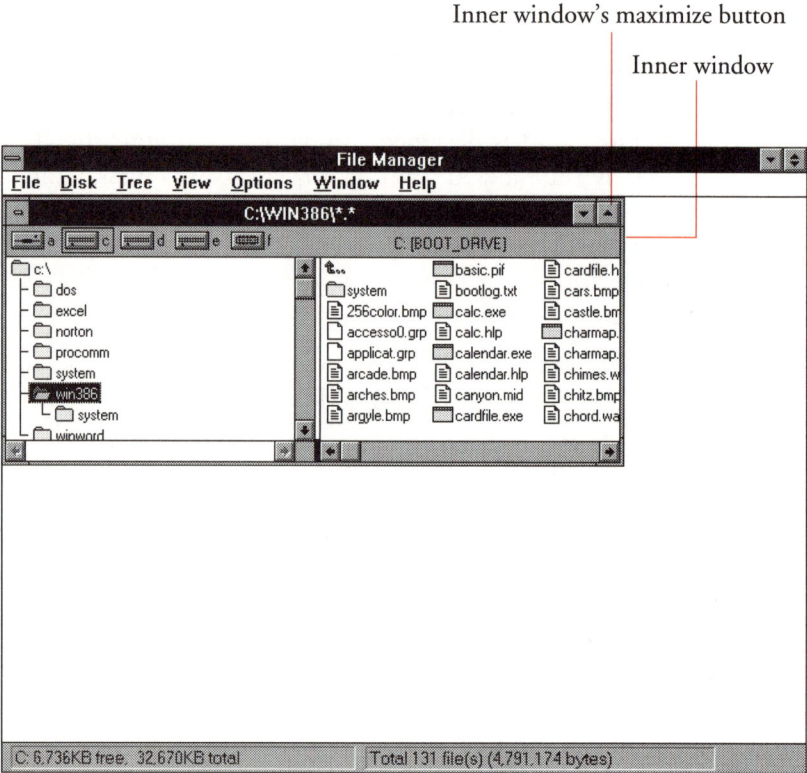

*Figure 3-1* The File Manager window starts as an outer window containing an inner window.

5. Click on the inner window's maximize button (located in the upper right corner of the inner window and labeled with an up arrow).

The inner window expands and merges with the outer window so you see a single window with a full inner workspace, as shown in Figure 3-2.

Volume icons

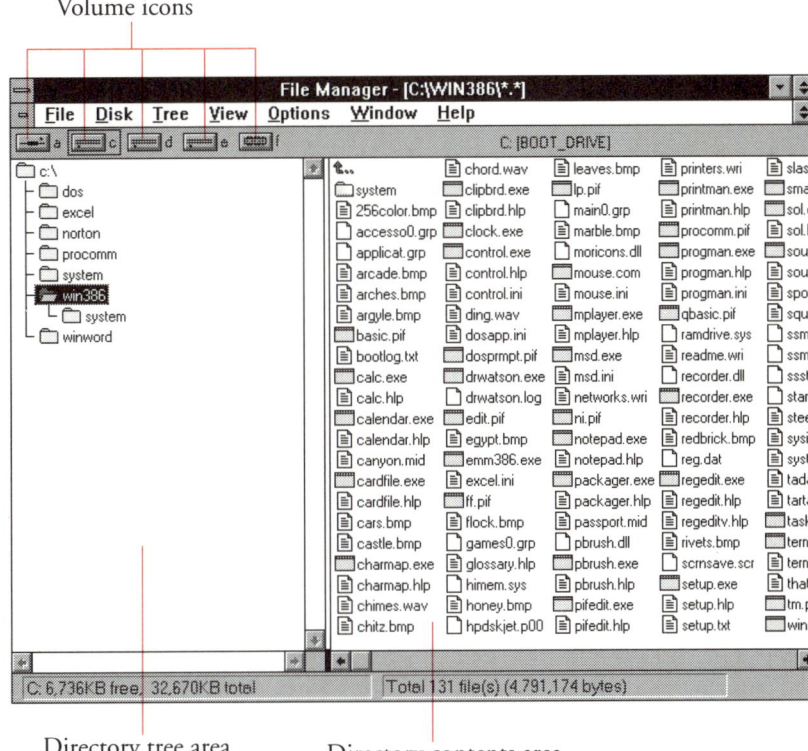

Directory tree area          Directory contents area

*Figure 3-2* The File Manager displays information about files and their locations on disks.

File Manager shows information about files in three main areas:

- The *volume icon* area, which shows you what disk drives and other storage devices are available to your computer
- The *directory contents* area, which shows the contents of different groups of files
- The *directory tree* area, which shows you how files are organized on a storage device

# The Volume Icon Area

The word *volume* is a generic term for a data storage device. A floppy disk is a volume; a hard disk is a volume; a CD-ROM drive is a volume; and so is another computer available to you over a computer network. If you have a typical computer, you have at least two volumes, listed in the volume icon area as *a* and *c*. *a* stands for A:, the floppy disk drive built into the computer; C: is the internal hard disk drive. If you have two floppy disk drives, the second floppy disk drive may appear as the icon *b*.

To help you identify volumes, File Manager uses a different icon for each type of storage device, as shown in Figure 3-3.

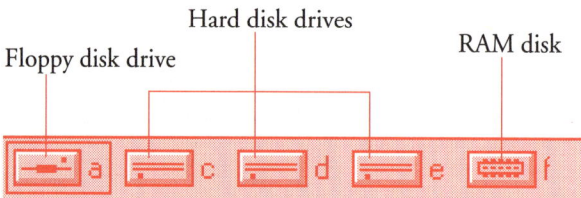

Hard disk drives

Floppy disk drive

RAM disk

*Figure 3-3* File Manager uses different icons to mark types of volumes.

### File Manager Shows More Hard Disks Than My Computer Has!

You *know* you only have one hard disk drive built into your computer, but when you run File Manager, it shows two or even more hard disk volumes in the volume icon area! What gives? Sleight of hand—or at least sleight of computer.

When your hard disk drive is first set up in your computer, MS-DOS offers an option to *partition* the hard disk drive, which divides the hard disk into several partitions, each of which acts as a separate volume. In effect, this turns one large hard disk drive into several smaller hard disk drives, because each disk partition appears as a separate volume to MS-DOS and Windows. For example, a single hard disk may be divided into three partitions: the first appears in File Manager on the right side of the volume icon area as *C:*, the second appears as *D:*, and the third appears as *E:*.

## Selecting a Volume

File Manager shows file information for one volume at a time—whichever volume is selected in the volume icon area. To look at files in a volume, you simply click on the volume you want to select it. File Manager outlines the volume to show that it's selected and then changes the contents of the directory tree and directory contents areas to show files and file structures on the newly selected volume. It also shows the label of the volume in the right side of the volume icon area. For example, if you select c, it might show *C:[BIGDISK]*. The name in brackets is the *volume label,* a name you can give to any volume to help you remember what it's for. Many volumes go unlabeled and won't show a name when you select them.

When you select a floppy disk drive in the volume icon area, File Manager checks the contents of the floppy disk inserted in the drive. If the drive is empty, File Manager prompts you to insert a floppy disk and try again. Try looking at the contents of a floppy disk following these steps:

1. Find a floppy disk that you know contains files—for example, the first of the floppy disks that came with Windows. Insert the disk label-side up and read-slot forward into your floppy disk drive. (If you have two floppy disk drives, insert the disk into the top disk drive.)

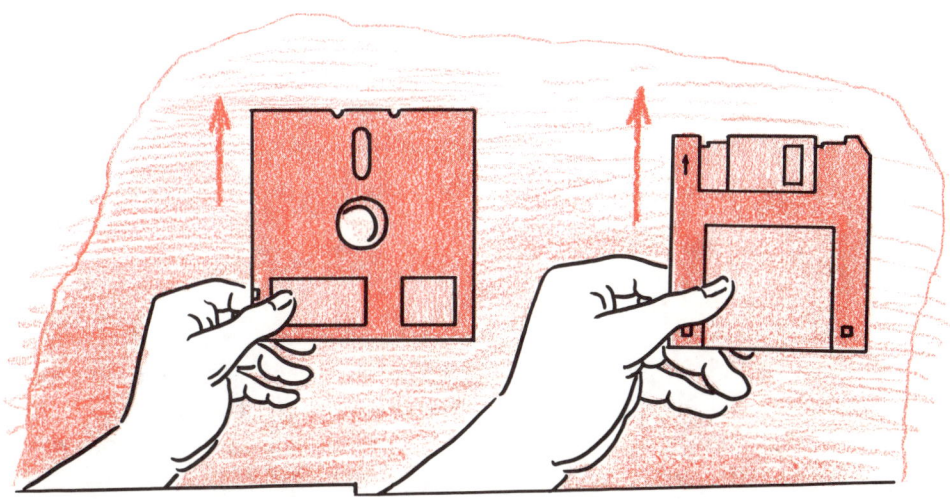

2.  Click on the volume icon for A: in the volume icon area to select the floppy disk drive.

    File Manager outlines the icon to show that it's selected, and displays the disk label to the right. The directory tree area shows the file organization on the floppy disk, and the directory contents area shows files from the floppy disk.

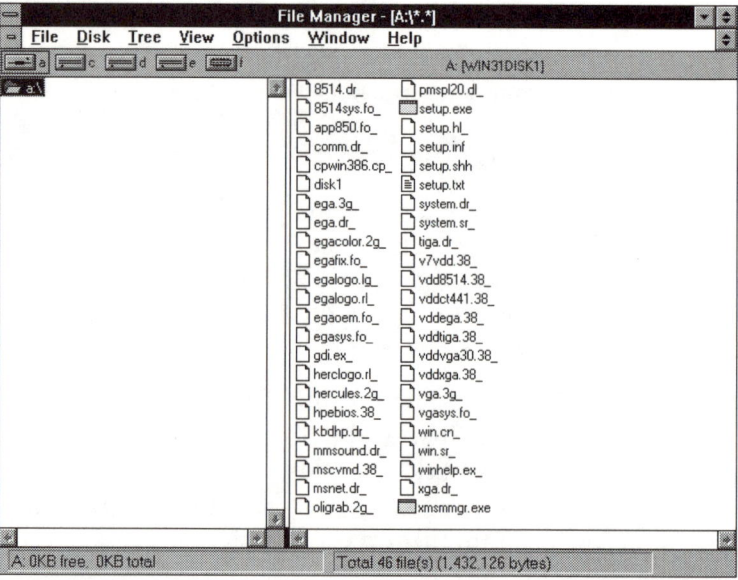

3.  Click on the volume icon for C: to select the hard disk drive. (If your system is set up differently, you may have to click on *d* or *e* to select the hard disk drive.)

    File Manager outlines the icon, displays the disk's label, and shows the hard disk's contents in the directory tree and directory contents areas.

## Directories and Directory Trees

The directory tree area of File Manager is an important tool for navigating through files as they're organized on a volume. To understand how it works, you must first understand the concept of a *directory,* an important method of organizing files.

Files can pile up on a disk just as easily as papers can bury a desktop. A typical hard disk can hold thousands of files, enough to make it very difficult to find a single file if you don't know its exact name. To organize papers on a desk, you bring in file folders and start sorting the papers into logical groups: personal letters, requests for donations, bills, income tax forms, tickets to Bermuda. You then put each group into a folder and label the folder, turning the large pile of papers into a much smaller pile of organized folders.

You use directories to organize files on a disk in the same way. You group files logically and store each group in its own directory, which you then give a meaningful name such as "letters" or "reports." By putting files in directories, you can find files more easily because you'll know where to look. Instead of searching through thousands of files for that letter you wrote to the editor, you can go to the directory Letters and look through fewer than a hundred files.

If a hundred letters still seems like too many files to plow through, you'll be happy to know that you can put directories within directories, just as you can put folders within folders for desk paper organization. For example, you might divide up the files in the Letters directory into three new directories: Personal, Business, and Editor (if you like to write to the papers frequently). When it comes time to look for that last letter to the editor, you look on your disk and find the Letters directory. When you look inside it, you find three directories and open the Editor directory, where you find the letters you've written to the editor. You can look through them until you've found the file you want. Figure 3-4 shows the structure of the directories for this example.

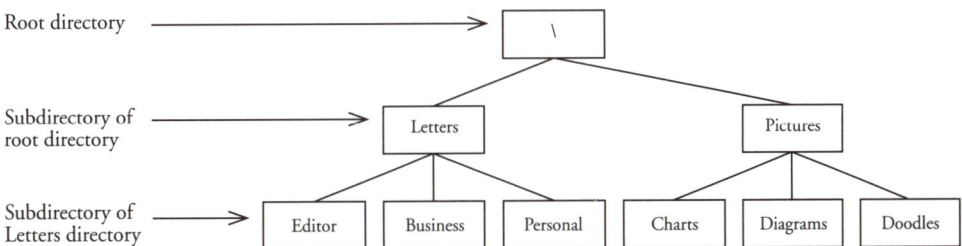

*Figure 3-4* A directory tree shows the structure of directories contained on a disk.

Directory structures are usually shown branching from the top down like an upside down tree and are called directory trees because they show how directories are organized in a tree-like structure rooted on the disk. The top directory (the volume itself) is called the *root directory* because all other directories are placed within it, so the directory tree grows out of it. The root directory is always named "\" (for no particular reason—it's just convention for computers running MS-DOS). A directory stored within another directory is called a *subdirectory*. In the last example, Editor is a subdirectory of Letters.

Any directory can contain files, subdirectories, or a mixture of both. For example, the Editor directory might contain a subdirectory named Times for letters to the *Times*, another named Midnight Tattler for letters concerning national politics, and a flush of miscellaneous letter files that aren't addressed to either publication.

If the ideas of files, directories, and directory trees seem to grow out of the realm of easy understanding, just remember that they very closely parallel papers, folders, and filing cabinets in the real world. The root directory is the room in which you sit. A filing cabinet in the room is a directory, and each drawer in the filing cabinet is a subdirectory. The folders in a drawer are subdirectories of the drawer, and the papers in a folder (or loosely tossed in a drawer or even thrown on the floor!) are all files because they contain stored information.

There is one important difference between paper files and computer files: You can have a practically infinite number of subdirectory levels on your computer—subdirectories within subdirectories within subdirectories within subdirectories, ad nauseum. If you try that with paper, you'll end up with split folders and sagging drawers.

With the idea of a directory tree planted firmly in mind, try looking at the directory tree of your hard disk drive using these steps:

1. If a hard disk drive icon isn't already selected, click on it to select it.

   The directory tree area shows directories contained on the hard disk.

2. Choose *Expand All* from the Tree menu in File Manager's menu bar.

   File Manager shows the full structure of the directory tree on your hard disk, which includes every subdirectory of every subdirectory as shown in Figure 3-5.

## A Pathname Can Take You Right There

A directory tree has one potential drawback for finding a file: you can't find a file by simply knowing its name. You must also know in which directory it's stored, not always a simple fact if that directory is a subdirectory stored in other subdirectories. To make finding a file simple, Windows often shows you a *pathname* to the file. Think of a pathname as a set of directions to a file that starts with the storage volume, proceeds from the root directory down to each subdirectory, and ends with the file's name—all pasted together in one string of characters.

For an example, look at this pathname:

**c:\writepro\letters\personal\elijah\howdo**

The "c:" at the beginning tells you to look on volume C: (probably your hard drive). The first backslash (\) is the root directory of the drive, and "writepro" after it tells you to look in the directory Writepro. The three directory names following, all separated by backslashes, are the levels of subdirectories you have to look into: first the Letters subdirectory, where you'll find the Personal subdirectory, where you'll find the Elijah subdirectory. The last word in the pathname is the name of the file you want in the directory Elijah. It's named "howdo".

You can also read a pathname backwards to get a feeling for a file's location: "It's the file 'howdo' located in the directory 'elijah', which is located in the directory 'personal' found in the directory 'letters' found in the directory 'writepro', which is found in the root directory of hard disk drive 'C:'". A mouthful, but you get the idea.

Root directory —————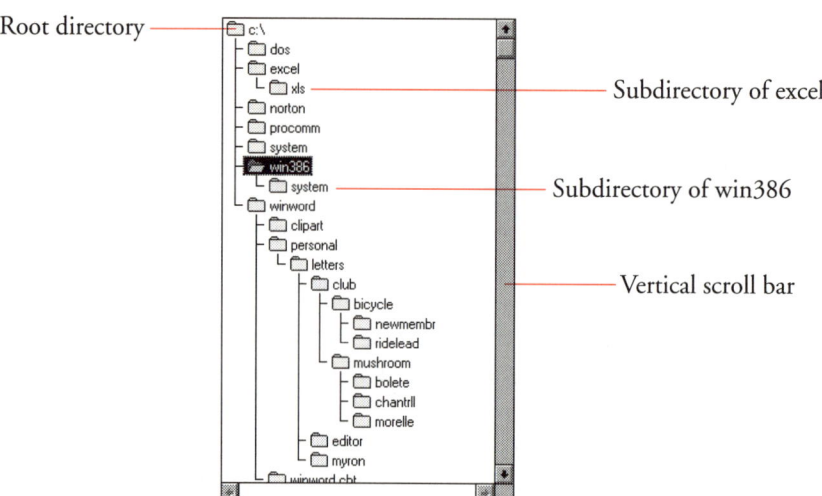

Subdirectory of excel

Subdirectory of win386

Vertical scroll bar

*Figure 3-5* The directory tree grows from the top of the window down, and shows subdirectories indented to the right of the directory in which they're contained.

3.  If the directory tree extends beyond the bottom of the window, use the vertical scroll bar to the right of the directory tree area to scroll the tree up and down to see its full length.

4.  Move to the top of the tree and double-click on *c:\.*

All of the root directory's subdirectories and their subdirectories disappear, leaving only the root directory in the tree.

5. Double-click once again on the root directory icon.

The root directory's subdirectories appear (but not the sub-directories' subdirectories).

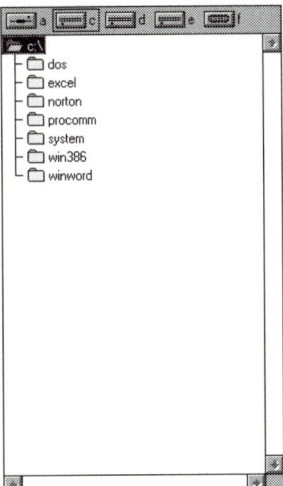

6. Find the directory labeled *windows* and double-click on it. (*windows* is the directory containing all Windows files. If you have Windows installed on a machine with a 80386 or 80486 central processor, the directory may be named *win386* instead.)

The tree expands to show the subdirectories of the Windows directory.

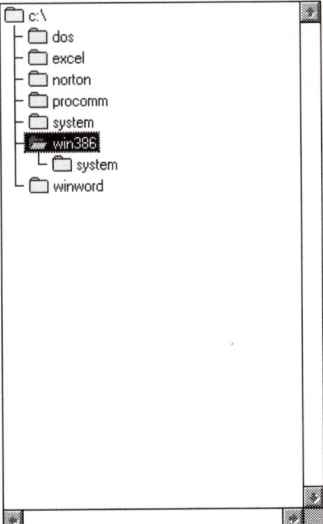

7. Single-click on the icon for the subdirectory System to select it.

    File Manager shows the contents of the System directory in the directory contents area in the right half of the window.

When you worked with the directory tree in the last example, you should have noticed some important facts:

- Double-clicking on a directory icon alternately reveals and then hides its subdirectories. Use this feature to selectively hide and reveal parts of the directory tree.

- Single-clicking *or* double-clicking selects a directory. The directory contents area to the right shows the contents of the selected directory.

To work best with the directory tree, you double-click your way through levels of directories until you find the directory you want, then select the directory so you can see its contents.

### How Do You Measure File Sizes?

Files are measured in *bytes,* a unit of storage capacity just large enough to store one character of a document (*a, M, q, 5,* or *9,* for random example). Because most files require thousands or even millions of bytes, they're often described in *kilobytes* (*K* for short), which are roughly one thousand bytes, and *megabytes* (*megs* or *M* for short), which are roughly one million bytes. If you see a file described as 20.45K in size, you know it's approximately 20,450 bytes large. When a hard disk is listed as having 120 megs of space, you know it can store approximately 120,000,000 bytes of information—enough space to store more than 2,000 times the number of characters in this book.

*(continued)*

> *How Do You Measure File Sizes? (continued)*
>
> A kilobyte is actually 1,024 bytes, exactly, because computers deal with numbers in powers of two, and 1,024 is two to the tenth power ($2^{10}$). Likewise, a megabyte is actually 1,048,576 (two to the twentieth power) bytes exactly. Don't worry about the precise values, though, and leave exactitude to your precision-loving computer. It's enough to think of 1K as 1,000 bytes and 1M as 1,000,000 bytes.

# Directory Contents

When File Manager shows the contents of a directory in the directory contents area, it lists files in columns that read like newspaper columns—read the columns from left to right. If there are more files than the area can display, use the horizontal scroll bar at the bottom of the area to scroll right to see more columns of file names.

File Manager normally lists files in alphabetical order by their file names. If there are subdirectories in the directory, they're also listed in alphabetical order and appear before the files. To help you see clearly which names in the list are subdirectories and which are files, File Manager puts a small icon before each name. The icons not only identify subdirectories, but show different types of files as well. The icons, as shown in Figure 3-6, are:

*Figure 3-6* File Manager uses file icons to identify different types of files.

- **Directory Icon** Used to mark a subdirectory
- **Program File Icon** Used to mark a file containing a program (such as Notepad or File Manager, for example)

- **Document File Icon**  Used to mark a file that contains data created while using a program (a letter created in Notepad, for example)

- **System File Icon**  Used to mark a file that contains data used by MS-DOS or Windows for running your computer system. (You should have no need to work directly with system files. They're like taxes—necessary to keep things running, but not something you want to be personally involved with.)

- **Generic File Icon**  Used to mark any file that doesn't fit the other three file categories.

As you browse through files in the directory contents area, you can see more information about a file by using File Manager's features. Try them by following these steps:

1. Click on the directory *windows* (or *win386*) in the directory tree to select it and show its contents in the directory contents area.

2. Click on the filename *calc.exe* in the directory contents area to select the file.

   File Manager highlights the file and displays the file's size (*42,928 bytes*) in the lower left corner of the window.

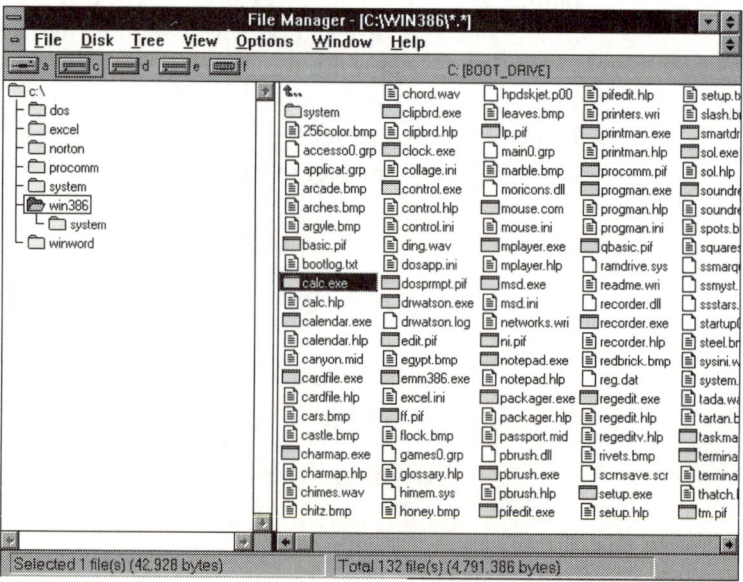

3.  Choose *All File Details* from the View menu.

The directory contents area changes to show the files listed in a single column (as shown in Figure 3-7). You can scroll through the column using the vertical scroll bar to its right.

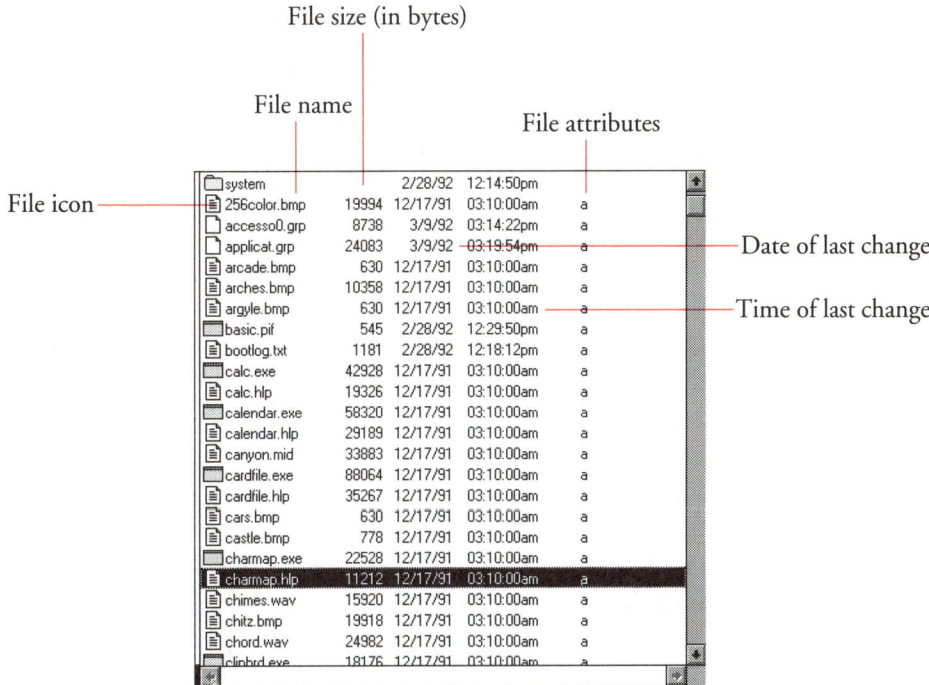

File size (in bytes)

File name

File attributes

File icon

Date of last change

Time of last change

*Figure 3-7* File Manager can display details about each file in a directory.

Each column in the area shows different information about the file. The first and second columns are the file icon and the file name. The third column shows the file's size in bytes. The fourth and fifth columns show the date and time when the file was last changed, and the sixth column shows the attributes of the file (file properties such as its system status that you don't need to be concerned with for everyday work).

4.  Choose *Name* from the View menu to return the directory contents area to its previous state.

## Looking for a File

If you're looking for a file and know its location and name, it's a simple matter to open the right directories and see the file listed in the File Manager window. If you don't know the exact location, you can browse through the directories (an activity that computer jocks affectionately refer to as "traversing the directory tree"). Try searching for the file mouse.ini using these steps:

1. If necessary, click on the directory *windows* in the directory tree area to select it and look at its contents in the directory contents area.

   File Manager sorts file names in alphanumeric order, so that *mouse.ini* should appear in the middle of the file list if it's in this directory (which it shouldn't be).

2. Double-click on the subdirectory *system* at the top of the directory contents area (*not* the *system* in the directory tree area).

   The directory contents area changes to show the contents of *system*, and the directory tree shows *system* highlighted. *mouse.ini* should appear in the file list—you've found it! Now return to the original directory.

3. Double-click on the arrow icon (followed by dots) that appears at the very top of the file list.

   The directory contents area shows the contents of the directory *windows*.

Notice that in the last example you moved through the directory tree without using the directory tree display area. The arrow and the subdirectory icons in the contents area move you up and down the tree without the need for the directory tree area. The arrow is called the *parent directory arrow* because it returns you to the *parent directory* of the current directory. (The parent directory is the next directory up the directory tree from the current directory—just as your parents are the next level up the family tree from you.)

# Starting Programs with File Manager

Now that you've used File Manager to explore disk contents, directory trees, and file lists, you may wonder just *why* you'd want to do so. Part of the answer is that you can clean up a disk with File

Manager—reorganizing files, creating and moving directories, erasing unnecessary directories and files, and similar tasks that you'll learn in Chapter 7. Another part of the answer is that you can use File Manager to start programs that you can't start with Program Manager.

Program Manager shows you groups of program files that you can double-click to start programs. The programs you see there are only those that have been specially set up to appear in Program Manager. Many programs on your disks may not appear at all in Program Manager.

That's where File Manager comes in. By exploring directory trees, you can find program files and start programs directly through File Manager—programs that you might not even see in Program Manager.

Try the technique of starting a program with File Manager by finding and starting Notepad. Its pathname is c:\windows\notepad .exe, which means that you'll find it in the Windows program directory on hard disk drive C: (unless you have Windows installed on a different volume, in which case it might be hard disk drive D:, E:, or another volume). Follow these steps:

1. If necessary, click on the icon *windows* in the directory tree to see the contents of the Windows directory.

2. Find the file *notepad.exe* in the directory contents area. (You may have to use the horizontal scroll bar to scroll right to see the file.)

3. Double-click on the file name *notepad.exe*.

   Notepad starts, and you see the Notepad window open on the screen with an empty document, ready to start work.

4. Double-click on the control-menu box in the upper left corner of the Notepad window to quit Notepad and close the window.

When you start a program the way you just did, or by using Program Manager, the program opens a window with a blank document ready for you to start a new project. If you want to resume work on a previously saved document, you use commands in the program's window to find the document file and load it into the program so you can see its contents. File Manager offers a shortcut if you've found a document file and want see it immediately displayed in the appropriate program: you double-click on the document file. Windows starts the program you need and shows your document file instead of a blank document. Try it now with these steps:

1. Find the file *bootlog.txt* in the directory contents area, then double-click it. (bootlog.txt is a file containing text created by Windows.)

   Notepad opens, and displays the contents of the document file bootlog.txt. Notice that the title bar of Notepad reads *Notepad - BOOTLOG.TXT*, which shows that it's displaying bootlog.txt.

2. Double-click on the control-menu box in the Notepad window to quit Notepad.

That finishes this round with File Manager. You quit it just as you quit any other Windows program: double-click on its control-menu box or choose *Exit* from its File menu.

You've now used File Manager to explore disk contents and to work your way through a directory tree. You've seen how it displays files, and how you can use it to start programs from program files you find in its window. You'll come back to File Manager in Chapter 7, where you'll learn much more about it's powerful features. In the meantime, you've finished this first section of the book and should be able to use Windows to start the programs you need and look through disks to find files you need. In the next section, you start off by trying Windows features that are standard to all Windows programs.

# PART II

## WORKING WITH PROGRAMS

Now that you know how to run Windows and how to run programs within Windows, you'll find Part II interesting. It shows you first how to work within a typical Windows program, then goes on to show you how to arrange programs to your taste in Program Manager and how to run more than one program at a time. By the end of these three chapters, you should be an accomplished program starter and manager, and you should know enough to feel at home with the basics in any Windows program, no matter how new you are to the program.

# CHAPTER

# 4

# EXPLORING PROGRAMS

When you sit down to the wheel of a car, you expect some standard controls: a steering wheel, an accelerator pedal, turn signals, a brake, an ignition switch. Because almost all cars have these same controls, it's not hard to start up a rental car and drive it off, even though you've never driven that model of car before. You might have some difficulty getting the ventilation just right or tuning in a radio station, but as long as you can roll down the road you'll have time to figure them out later.

Windows imposes the same sort of control standards on Windows programs so that you can sit down to a new program and know immediately how to perform the basics. Although some of the specifics may be new and not so obvious (the equivalent of a 50-button car radio with a graphic equalizer), you should be able to issue commands, enter text, open and save files, and—when something stumps you—find the owner's manual so you'll know how to handle the unknowns. In this chapter, you see how to use standard Windows controls so you'll feel comfortable behind the wheel of any Windows program.

## Using Menus

To work with a program, you must be able to give it commands. And to issue a command in a Windows program, you use menus. Although the standard technique for choosing a menu command is very simple (click on a menu name to open the menu, click on a command name to issue the command), you'll find some menu nuances that aren't quite as obvious—and are very useful.

The best way to get a feel for menu nuances is to try them out. Take a minute now to start a typical Windows application where you can experiment:

1. Turn on your computer and start Windows, if you haven't done so already.

2. Use the Program Manager to start Write, the simple word processor that comes with Windows. (You should find it in the Accessories program group.)

Whenever you open a menu, you find a list of commands. Each command is called a *menu item.* Windows shows menu items with some subtle differences that give you information before you choose the command.

## Dimmed Menu Items

You may find some menu items that look dimmed or grayed out in contrast to other items listed in bold black letters. For example, open the Edit menu in Write (shown in Figure 4-1) and look at the items there.

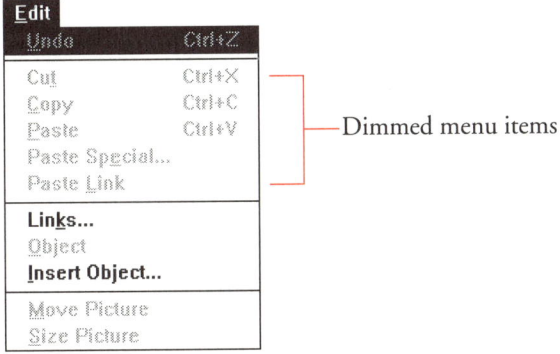

*Figure 4-1* A dimmed menu item shows that a command isn't currently available.

Dimmed items are unavailable commands. You can't choose them even if you click on them, because the command won't work in the present circumstances. For example, the command Copy won't work unless you have some text available to copy, so the Copy menu item is dimmed when you have an empty document in a program. Once circumstances change so the command is appropriate, the menu item is undimmed; it appears in dark letters so you can choose it. For example, if you add text to a document and then select the text, you can choose the Copy command.

## Menu Item Groups

Some menus—especially long menus—insert horizontal lines between menu items to break up items into logical groups. For example, open the File menu in Write. You'll see three groups, as shown in Figure 4-2. The first group offers commands that move document files in and out of Write, the second group offers commands that control document printing, and the third group (consisting of one lonely item) lets you quit Write.

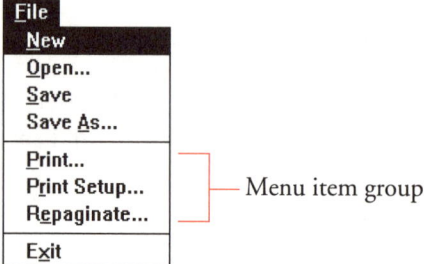

— Menu item group

*Figure 4-2* A menu item group offers a group of logically related commands

## Toggled Menu Items

Some menu items alternately turn a feature on or off whenever you choose the item. These items are called toggled menu items because they work like a toggle switch that you flip on and off. The first time you choose the command, you turn the feature on, and Windows adds a mark before the command (usually a checkmark as shown in Figure 4-3) so you know the feature is on. The next time you choose the command, you turn the feature off, and the mark disappears.

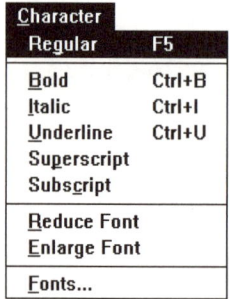

*Figure 4-3* A toggled menu item turns a feature on and off.

Follow these steps to try toggling items:

1. Open the Character menu in Write and choose *Bold.*

2. Open the Character menu again.

   You see a checkmark before *Bold,* which shows that the option is now turned on.

3. Choose *Italic* from the Character menu.

4. Open the Character menu again.

You see a checkmark before both *Italic* and *Bold*, showing that both options are turned on.

5. Choose *Bold* from the Character menu and then choose *Italic* from the Character menu.

After you choose each option a second time, the checkmark disappears, showing that the option is turned off.

You'll occasionally find a menu item group of related toggled items. Whenever you turn one item on by choosing it, the other items are automatically turned off. This works something like air conditioning temperature buttons; when you punch the button for "Freezing," the button for "Chilly" pops out because you can't set the temperature to "Freezing" and "Chilly" at the same time. To see an example, open the Paragraph menu in Write. The second item group there has four items: *Left, Center, Right,* and *Justify.* You can only turn one of these on at a time.

## Menu Items That Open Dialog Boxes

Many commands you issue to a program require additional information before the program can carry them out: How many pages do you want to print? What file do you want to open? How fast do you want to send information over the modem? These commands are marked with an ellipsis (...) following the menu item, which means that Windows opens a dialog box (as shown in Figure 4-4) when you choose that item. For an example, choose *Print* from the File menu to open the Print dialog box, then press the Esc key on your keyboard to close the dialog box.

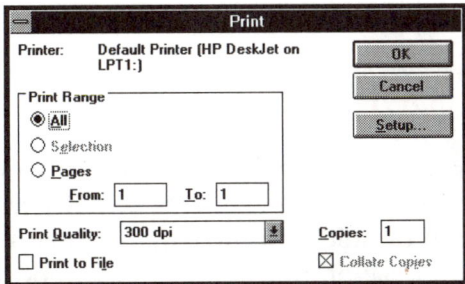

*Figure 4-4* A dialog box allows you to give additional information necessary to carry out a command.

Think of a dialog box as a small form to fill out. You enter text, click on buttons, set options, and give any other necessary information. When you're finished, click on the OK button, and the program accepts your information and closes the dialog box. If you get cold feet and want to close the dialog box without any effect (getting rid of any information you might have entered), click on the Cancel button or simply press the Esc key.

---

**If You Just Hate to Open Menus...**

Sometimes it's a tremendous distraction to open a menu to issue a command. You're in the middle of typing an inspired love letter; you've just figured out how many pico-hectares there are in a square mile; you don't want to lose your train of thought. Reaching over for the mouse, rolling and clicking, and then coming back to your work is just too much to bear. Fear not. There's an answer: keyboard shortcuts.

You may notice that some menu items are followed by cryptic notes such as *Alt+Enter* or *F4*. These are reminders that the command has a keyboard shortcut you can press to issue the command instead of choosing it from a menu. For example, the standard editing command Cut almost always has the keyboard shortcut Ctrl+X, which means that if you press the Ctrl and X keys together, you ask the program to cut without ever opening a menu. Very useful... and not so likely to interrupt your flow of work.

---

# Working Your Way through a Dialog Box

Once you open a dialog box, you'll most likely find an array of Windows' standard controls: buttons, check boxes, lists, text boxes, and others that you can twiddle with the mouse and keyboard. All are designed to get information from you, and all work the same way from program to program.

## Command Buttons

The most common (and simplest!) control is the command button, a button you click on to issue a command. You've already used a command button to quit Windows: you clicked on *OK* to confirm that you were ready to quit.

You don't always need to click on a command button to use it. If you see one command button in a group with outlined text in the button, you can simply press the Enter key to select the button and issue its command. This is a useful keyboard shortcut that can keep your hands on the keyboard and away from the mouse at awkward times.

## List Boxes

A list box (shown in Figure 4-5) offers a list of options from which you can choose. If the list is long, the box offers a scroll bar on the side so you can scroll up and down through the list to find the option you want. To select an item, you click on it. Windows highlights the option and unhighlights any other option that might be selected in the list box. To see what's selected in a list box, just look through it for the highlighted item.

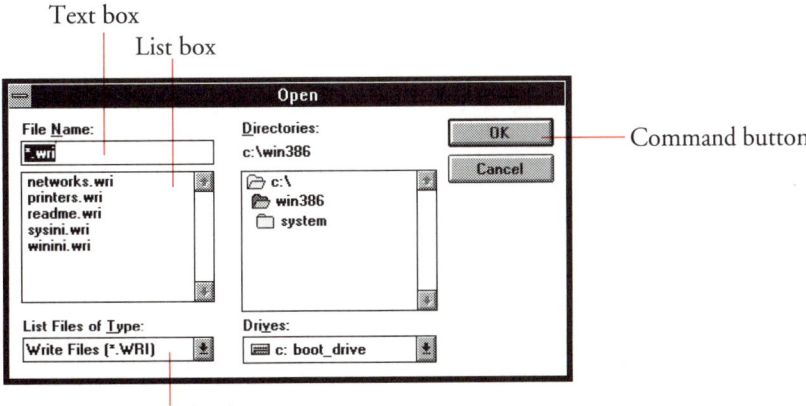

*Figure 4-5* The list box and the drop-down list box both offer a list of options from which you can choose. A text box allows you to enter an option from the keyboard. The command button executes a command when you click on it.

To see an example of a *list box*, choose *Open* from the File menu to open the Open dialog box. (If a dialog box opens and asks if you want to save changes to the untitled document we've been playing with, click *No*.) You'll find two list boxes there: one, on the left, with a list of file names; another, on the right, with a list of directory names. Try selecting a file name from the file name list: click on a name and see it highlighted.

## Drop-down List Boxes

Many dialog boxes save space by using a *drop-down list box* (shown in Figure 4-5) instead of a full-blown list box. A drop-down list box shows only a single option at a time; to see more, you click on it, much the same as clicking on a menu title. It opens to reveal a list of options—often with a scroll bar if the list is long. To select a new option, simply click on the option you want, and the list closes. The selected option appears in the closed drop-down list box.

Try one of the drop-down list boxes in Write's Open dialog box:

1. Choose *Open* from the File menu to open the Open dialog box (if it's not already open).

2. Click on the drop-down list box labeled *List Files of Type*.

    The list box opens.

3. Use the scroll bar on the side of the list box to scroll down to the bottom, then click on the option All Files (*.*).

    The list box closes and your selected option—*All Files (*.*)*— appears in the closed list box.

## Text Boxes

Clicking on options doesn't always give enough information. If a dialog box needs text from you, it presents a text box where you can type. The text box may be empty or already filled with text (usually information that the program assumes you want there). If the text box is full, you can modify its text, or you can erase it completely and type in something new.

To use a text box, move the pointer into the box and click. The insertion point appears: a thin, blinking, vertical line. If you click in the middle of existing text, the insertion point appears between letters—wherever you clicked with the tip of the pointer.

To enter text, type at the keyboard. Characters appear at the insertion point location. You can insert new characters by pressing character keys (X, H, 4, and so on), or you can delete existing characters by pressing Backspace (a good way to fix typing errors or to get rid of existing text).

Try using the text box in Write's Open dialog box:

1. Move the pointer to the right end of the text box labeled *File Name* and click.

   The insertion point appears at the end of the text in the box.

2. Press the Backspace key until you erase all the text from the box, then type in the name `anyfile`. You can use Backspace to correct any errors you make.

3. Click on the Cancel button to close the Open dialog box without taking any action on the settings you've made there.

Once you type text in a text box, you usually press Enter or click on a command button to make your text take effect. One speed tip: If the text in the text box is highlighted, all you need to do to replace it is start typing. The first keystroke of your typing erases the highlighted text. A dialog box often opens with highlighted text in a text box so you can replace it easily if you'd like to.

## Option Buttons

Option buttons look simple (see Figure 4-6), and they are. They usually appear in groups, like a cluster of buttons on a radio, each button with a label to the side. To turn on an option button in a group, you click on the button, and a dot appears within the button to show that it's turned on. Only one option button in a group can be turned on at a time; when you click on one button to turn it on, all the other buttons in the group turn off.

To try a set of option buttons, choose *Page Layout* from Write's Document menu to open the Page Layout dialog box. At the bottom, you'll find two option buttons that set the type of measurements used in Write: either inches (*inch*) or centimeters (*cm*). Notice that when you click on one, the other turns off. Click on *Cancel* to close the dialog box when you're finished.

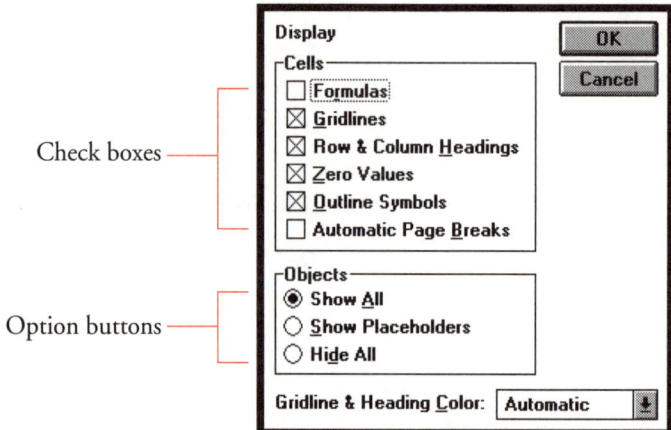

*Figure 4-6* Option buttons let you choose one option from a group, while check boxes let you turn on as many features as you want from a group.

## Check Boxes

Check boxes provide a quick way for you to turn features on and off. When you click on a check box, you toggle it on or off: one click turns it on (an *x* appears in the box), another turns it off (the box clears). Although check boxes often appear in a group, they aren't exclusive like option buttons; turning on one check box won't automatically turn off the other check boxes. This allows you to turn on check box features simultaneously.

To try check boxes, choose *Save As* from Write's File menu to open the Save As dialog box. You'll see a single check box—*Backup* —on the right side of the box, which you can turn on and off by clicking. Click on *Cancel* to close the dialog box when you're finished.

## Entering Text

Although you give commands to a program with menus and dialog boxes, you'll probably find that you do most of your real work by entering text in a window's workspace: typing a letter in a word processor, entering data in a data base program, typing figures for a spreadsheet, and so on. The techniques you use to enter text are—with some variations for advanced features—standard from program to program.

## The Insertion Point

The *insertion point* shows you where you're entering text in the workspace. It's a thin vertical line so that it can fit in between characters, and it blinks on and off so that you can find it in the midst of a page full of text. You should see it blinking now in the upper left corner of Write's workspace.

Don't confuse the insertion point with the pointer. The pointer shows where your mouse is working, and you move it with the mouse; the insertion point shows where the keyboard is working, and you move it with keystrokes as you type text. You can also move the insertion point with the four *cursor keys* on your keyboard, each labeled with an arrow. When you press the up or down cursor keys, you move the insertion point up or down by one line. When you press the left or right cursor keys, you move the insertion point left or right by one character.

If you want to quickly move the insertion point a long distance, point to a new location in text with the pointer and then click, just as you did to select a text box for typing.

## Typing Text

Typing text is more a matter of finger coordination than of any special knowledge: you press character keys to spell out the words and numbers you want to enter, and the text appears on the screen, as the insertion point sweeps from left to right. Try it now:

1. Type a few sentences of text without pressing the Enter key. Anything will do—even gibberish—as long as you break it up with spaces.

    The insertion point moves from left to right as you type. When you reach the end of the line, the insertion point automatically jumps to the beginning of the next line.

2. Continue typing until you have at least three lines of text.

3. Press the up arrow key several times.

   The insertion point moves up one line each time you press it until it reaches the top line.

4. Press the left cursor key.

   The insertion point moves left through the text.

5. Type some new text while the insertion point is located in the middle of existing text.

   The text you type appears at the insertion point location, while existing text is pushed to the right and then down to the next line to make room.

6. Move the pointer to the end of the last line of text and then click.

   The insertion point jumps to the click location.

If you're used to typewriters, you'll see some distinct differences here. One of the most convenient is *word wrap,* a feature that most —but not all—Windows programs have. When you type to the end of a line in a program with word wrap, the insertion point automatically jumps to a new line without breaking up any words at the line's end. If you enter text in a program without word wrap, the text may continue off the side of the window, out of sight. You have to press Enter at the end of a line to start a new line. With word wrap, you don't need to press Enter except at the end of a paragraph.

When you move the insertion point into existing text and start typing, you insert text and push existing text to the right. If you press the Backspace key, characters disappear to the left of the insertion point, and following text moves backward to fill in the space. This makes it very easy to revise text in the workspace: just move the insertion point to the revision spot and then insert or delete characters.

## Selecting Text

You select text in Windows for the same reason you select objects: you want to point it out as something to be affected by the next action you take. Selecting an object is simple—you point and click. Selecting text is almost as easy—you move the pointer to one end of the text you want, drag the pointer to the other end of the text, still holding down the mouse button, and release the mouse button there. All the text between the two spots is highlighted so you can see what text is selected.

If you want to select a block of text that stretches far beyond the top, bottom, or sides of the workspace, you click once to position the insertion point at one end of the text block, scroll the text with scroll bars, point to the second end of the text block, hold down the Shift key, then click again. All text between the click and the Shift+click is selected. This Shift-click technique is called *extended selection,* and is useful throughout Windows.

Try selecting text in your sample now:

1. Move the pointer to the beginning of the first line, then drag through the first three words, releasing the mouse button at the end of the third word.

   The first three words of text are highlighted, showing they're selected.

2. Click at the beginning of the text.

   The insertion point appears at the beginning of the text, and the selected text is no longer selected.

3. Move the pointer to the end of the text, hold down the Shift key, and click.

   All text between the first click location and the Shift+click location is highlighted.

Notice that whenever you want to *deselect* text (remove its highlight), you simply click anywhere in the workspace. You can also drag in a new location to select a different block of text.

The idea behind text selection is that once you've selected text, you can affect it with further actions. For example, if you press the Backspace key, all selected text is deleted at a single stroke. Or if you start to type new text, all selected text is replaced with your new text. If you select an editing command from a menu, the command affects the selected text. Try it now:

1. Press the Backspace key.

   All text in the text block disappears from the document.

2. Choose *Undo Editing* from the Edit menu.

   All deleted text appears back in the document.

## Cutting, Copying, and Pasting Text

Three editing commands common to almost every Windows program are *Cut, Copy,* and *Paste.* Cut removes selected text from a document and puts it into an area of computer memory called the *clipboard.* The clipboard can hold one cut piece of text at a time. Each time you use the Cut command, the clipboard erases whatever it's holding and uses the newly cut text to replace it—so before you use Cut, be sure you don't need the old text in the clipboard.

The Paste command inserts the contents of the clipboard into a document at the insertion point location, just as if you typed it there. It doesn't remove the clipboard contents though—it just copies it—so you can keep pasting the same clipboard contents over and over again into a text area.

The Copy command is a variation of the Cut command; it puts selected text into the clipboard, but doesn't delete the original selected text in the document. (It does, however, delete the clipboard's previous contents to make way for the copied text.)

You use these three commands together move text from one spot to another, to make quick copies of selected text, and to perform other quick editing functions. Because the clipboard carries text between separate Windows documents and programs, you'll find that you can copy text from one letter into a new letter, or from a word processor into a data base program—quite a timesaver if used properly!

Try Cut, Copy, and Paste now:

1. Select the first three words of your document.
2. Choose *Cut* from the Edit menu.

   The three selected words are cut from the document, and are stored (invisibly) in the clipboard.
3. Move the insertion point into the middle of the text remaining in the document, then choose *Paste* from the Edit menu.

   The three words you cut earlier are inserted into the document at the insertion point's location.
4. Choose *Paste* from the Edit menu two more times.

   Each time you choose *Paste,* you insert another copy of the three words stored in the clipboard.

# Handling Document Files

When you work in a Windows program, each project you create is called a document. A document can be a letter home in a word processor, an office budget in a spreadsheet program, or a list of wine bottles stored in a data base program. To keep your work from flashing away when you turn off the computer, you save it in a document file, which you can load again at another time to resume your work. Because saving, opening, and printing these files are standard operations in almost every Windows program, Windows uses standard commands (usually found in the File menu) to run them. Those commands are *Save*, *Open*, and *Print*.

## Saving a Document File

When you've finished work on a document, you save it to disk by choosing *Save* from the File menu. The Save As dialog box shown in Figure 4-7 opens. Although the dialog box may vary slightly from program to program, the basics are the same. You'll find a list where you can choose a drive, a list where you can choose a directory for saving, a list to show you existing files in a directory, and a text area where you can enter a file name for your document. The buttons on the side let you proceed with or cancel the save.

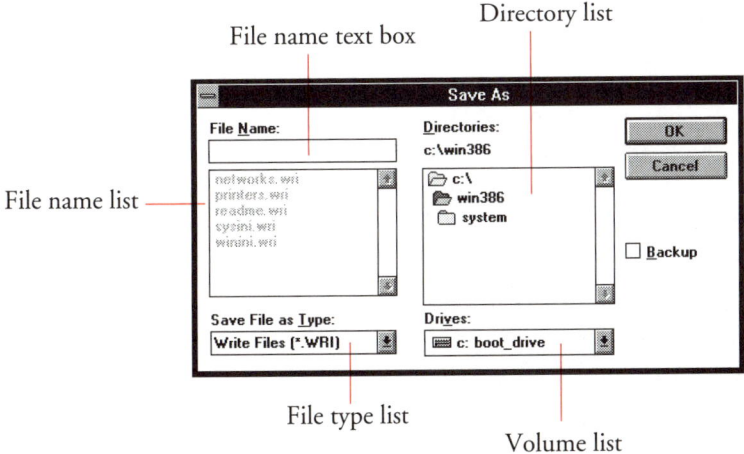

*Figure 4-7* The Save As dialog box lets you set a drive, directory and filename for your document file.

## Choosing a Drive and a Directory

Your first order of business is to choose a drive and a directory on that drive where you'll save the document. The Save As dialog box automatically proposes the drive and the directory where you started your program, but you can choose another drive, if you wish, from the Drives pull-down list and another directory from the Directories list. When you select a new drive, the Directories list changes to show you the directory tree from that disk. It's very similar to the tree you worked with in File Manager. Try it now:

1. Choose *Save* from the File menu to open the Save As dialog box.

2. Double-click on the directory *temp* in the Directories list to select that directory. If you don't have a directory called *temp*, just select *Windows*.

   The Temp directory icon opens up, and the directory name is highlighted to show that it's selected. The directory's path-name appears above the Directories list.

One note about choosing a directory: If you can't see the directory you want, you can double-click on any directory icon to see its sub-directories and then double-click on those subdirectories to see theirs, and so on. You work through the tree just as you did in File Manager, until you get to the directory where you want to save your document.

## Naming the Document

Once you've set a drive and a directory, you give your document a name by entering a name in the File Name text area. The file name list just below shows you what names are already used in the directory so you can avoid name duplication.

When you name a document, you must follow MS-DOS's standard naming conventions, which, unfortunately, are a little sticky. Here they are:

- The body of the name must be no longer than eight characters long.

- The name must start with a letter or a number, and can use any characters except a period (.), slash (/), brackets ([ ]), semi-

colon (;), equals sign (=), quotation mark ("), backslash (\),
colon (:), vertical bar (¦), or comma (,).

- You cannot use these names (they're reserved by MS-DOS):
CON, AUX, COM1, COM2, COM3, COM4, LPT1, LPT2,
LPT3, PRN, or NUL.

- You may add an *extension* to the name of one, two, or three
characters. The extension is added to the end of the body of
the name, and is separated from the body by a period. You use
the same set of characters for the extension that you use for
the body.

Forget the specifics, and remember these rules of thumb: use only
letters and numbers; don't use names that sound like devices connected to the computer; use up to eight characters for the body; use
up to three characters for the extension (if you choose to have one);
and put a period between an extension and the body of the name.
These file names are all acceptable:

CHARLIE   FORECAST.93  2TIMES.WRI

These file names aren't acceptable:

"GOOD".DOC (uses quotes)

ATTENTION.MEMO (too many characters in body and extension)

ANNOUNCE.DOC.89 (two extensions—only one is permitted)

Once you've entered the file name you want, click on the OK
button to save the document under that name in the directory and
disk that you set. If you get cold feet and don't want to save, click
on *Cancel* to close the dialog box without saving. Try saving now:

1. Enter the name `eraseme` in the File Name text area.
2. Click the OK button.

The Save As dialog box closes, and your document is saved in the
Temp directory under the name *eraseme.wri*. You can see the docu-
ment name in the Write window title bar. It reads *Write - ERASEME
.WRI*.

Notice that Write automatically appended the extension "wri" to
your file name. This identifies the document as one created in Write.
You can create your own extension if you want by adding one in the
File Name text area, but letting the program automatically add its
extension helps you later to identify document types by their file
name extensions.

## Saving a Document More Than Once

When you've given a document a file name and saved it, you don't have to work with the Save As dialog box the next time you save the document. When you choose *Save* from the File menu, the program saves your document to the same file name, erasing the old version of the document and saving the latest version. It's a wise idea to save your work this way every fifteen minutes or so; if the power to your computer suddenly goes out and you lose the document, you can start up again later, open your last-saved version of the document, and know that you haven't lost more than fifteen minutes of work.

If you revise an old document and decide that you'd like to keep the old version and save the new version in a new file, choose *Save As* from the File menu. It reopens the Save As dialog box so you can set a new disk, directory, or file name and save the document as a new file, leaving the old version of the document intact.

## Opening a Document

Once you've saved a document and either closed the document or quit the program, the document is no longer in the computer's memory. In order to work on it again, you must open the document using the Open command in the File menu.

When you choose *Open*, you see the Open dialog box shown in Figure 4-8. It looks a lot like the Save As dialog box, and works much the same. You choose a disk and a directory using the Drives and Directories lists, and the File Name list shows you the files contained in the selected directory. To load one of those files, click on it to select it and then click the OK button. Or, for speed, simply double-click on the file name. The dialog box closes and the document opens in the program's workspace.

Try closing your example document and then opening it:

1. Choose *New* from the File menu.

   Your old document closes automatically, and Write puts an empty new document in its window.

2. Choose *Open* from the File menu to open the Open dialog box.

3. Find the name *eraseme.wri* in the File Name list box and double-click on it.

The dialog box closes, and your document opens in the Write window.

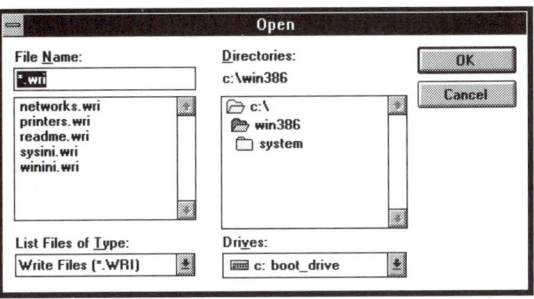

*Figure 4-8* The Open dialog box lets you look through disks and directories for the file you want to open.

One important fact to notice is that the File Name list in the Open dialog box doesn't always show every file contained in the current directory. It filters the files to show only those it thinks you're interested in. For example, if you're using Write, it shows only file names that end with the extension ".WRI". If you want to see other files, choose a file type from the List Files of Type drop-down list box. In Write, you'll find types that show documents created by other word processors. You'll also find *All Files*, which shows every file in the selected directory, regardless of its file name extension.

## Printing a Document

Getting your work out into the real world often requires printing it on a printer, another common task that uses a standard Windows procedure. To print a document, you first open it and then choose *Print* from the File menu, which opens up the Print dialog box (shown in Figure 4-9). This dialog box looks different from system to system, depending on the kind of printer attached. (Windows has a custom Print dialog box for each variety of printer that includes controls for the printer's special features, some of which are unique.)

Almost every kind of Print dialog box two common functions:

- **Copies** Sets the number of copies of your document that you want to print

- **Range** Sets the range of pages you want to print (for example, pages 2 to 5 of a fifteen-page report).

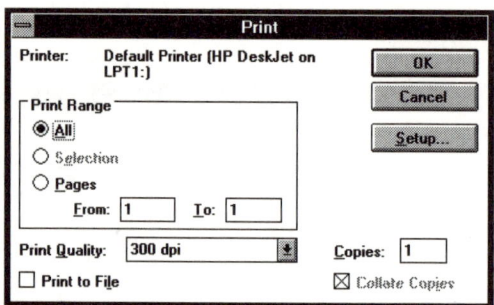

*Figure 4-9* The Print dialog box varies depending on your printer.

To set the number of copies you want to print, just enter the number in the Copies text box. To set the range, you can select one of three options:

- **All** Prints every page in the document
- **Selection** Prints only the text you have selected in the document (the text you see highlighted)
- **Pages** Prints a range of pages, which you must enter in the From and To text boxes.

For example, if you want to print four copies of pages 5-10 of a twenty-page report, you enter 4 in the Copies text box, select the Pages option, enter 5 in the From text box, and 10 in the To text box. Or if you want just one copy of page 5, you enter 1 in *Copies*, select the Pages option, and enter 5 in both the From and To text boxes.

Once you've set all the printing options you want (see your printer manual or the Windows manual for specifics on your printer's features), then click *OK* to start printing or *Cancel* if you get wet feet and want to leave the dialog box without printing. If you want to try printing now, follow these steps:

1. Turn on your printer and make sure it has paper and is ready for printing.
2. Choose *Print* from the File menu to open the Print dialog box.

3. Click the OK button.

   The Print dialog box closes, and your one-page document prints.

Notice that you didn't have to set any printing options in this example. The Print dialog box always opens with its options set to one copy of all pages. When you click *OK*, you accept those settings.

## Document Windows and Document Icons

Many Windows programs can only show one open document at a time. If you open a new document with another document already open, the program closes the open document first (after politely asking if you want to save your work first). Other Windows programs allow you to open more than one document at a time. To provide a separate work area for each open document, Windows uses a special type of window: the document window, which is one of two types of windows found in Windows.

The first—and most common—type of window is the *application window*. You're quite familiar with it; it's the window that opens when you start a program. It provides a menu bar for commands and a workspace where it can display and accept information. You can minimize, maximize, resize, and move an application window all over the desktop, and even drag it partially out of sight by taking it off the edge of the desktop.

The second type of window is a *document window,* which appears only within the workspace of an application window. You may want to think of the application window's interior as a sort of "private desktop" that supports document windows. You can minimize, maximize, resize, and move document windows, but never beyond the confines of its parent application window. If you minimize a document window to an icon, the icon appears within the application window. If you try to drag a document window outside the borders of the application window, it disappears at the application window's border, just as an application window disappears at the desktop's border.

In appearance, a document window (shown in Figure 4-10) looks almost exactly like an application window. It has standard buttons, borders, and a title bar that gives the name of the document file. There is one main difference to help you tell a document window from an application window: a document window has no menu bar; an application window does. If you want to give commands to affect the contents of a document window, you use the menus in the application window that contains the document window.

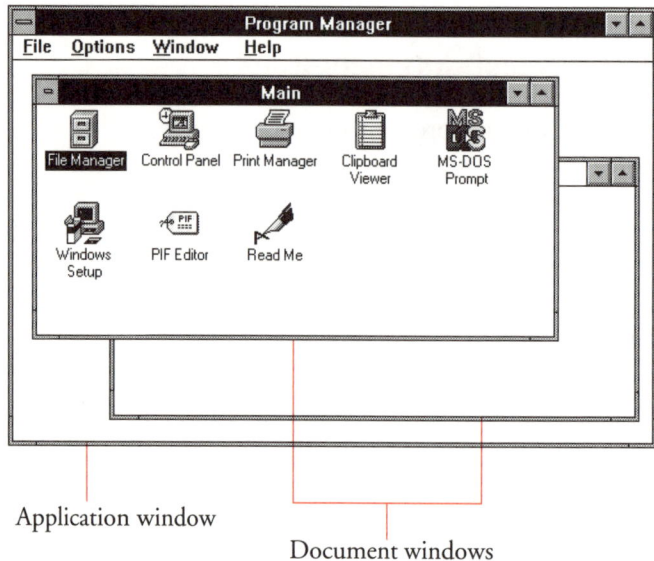

Application window

Document windows

*Figure 4-10* Document windows appear only within the confines of their parent application window.


## Manipulating Document Windows

You can manipulate a document window much as you do an application window: You move the window by dragging its title bar; you resize it by dragging one of its sides or corners; you reduce it to an icon by clicking on its minimize button; you increase it to full size by clicking on its maximize button. You'll find one difference when you maximize a document window: the window grows to fill the application window's workspace, and it merges with the application window, losing its own border and title bar. It retains only its control menu and its maximize button.

To detach a fully maximized document window from the application window so it's once again an independent entity, click on its maximize button. It shrinks to its previous size, its title bar and borders return, and you can see the workspace behind it.

## Multiple Document Windows

When you open several documents at one time in an application window, their windows usually overlap each other. The window on top —with a highlighted title bar—is the active window. It's the only window affected by any commands you choose from the application window's menu bar. You can make any other window the active window by clicking in that window; it comes to the front, and its title bar is highlighted.

If you have several document windows open at once, they can get cluttered, and you might have trouble finding the document you're looking for. If so, you can reduce some of them to icons by clicking on their minimize buttons. If you want to neatly arrange open document windows, you can use two commands from the Window menu: Tile and Cascade.

When you choose *Tile*, Windows sizes your document windows and arranges them like tiles on a floor so they fill the upper part of the application window as shown in Figure 4-11. No document window covers another document window, and a small strip appears at the bottom of the application window so you can see window icons there.

If you choose *Cascade* to organize the document windows, they're overlapped one on top of the other and cascaded from upper left to lower right, something like a deck of cards fanned out on a table. You can see the title bar of each window so you can quickly click on the one you want to bring to the front and make it the active window.

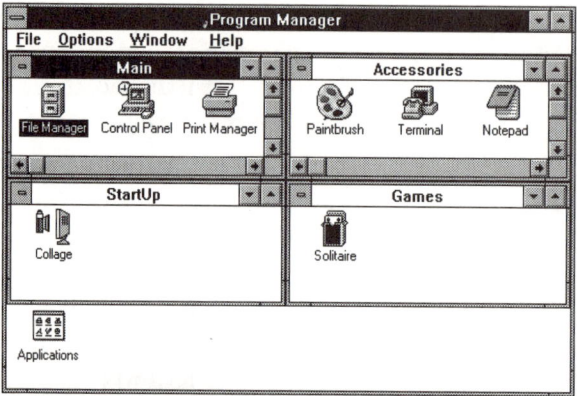

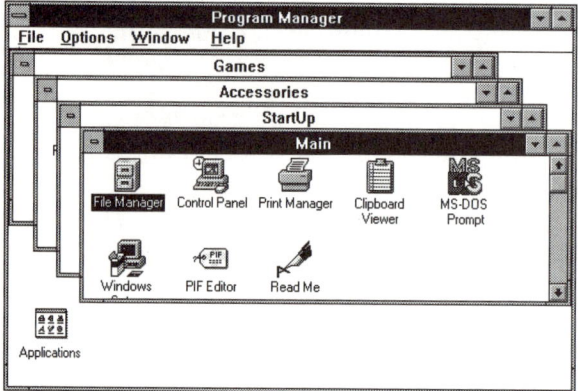

## Arranging Document Icons

You'll find one other useful command in the Window menu: Arrange Icons. This is particularly helpful if you've reduced many document windows to icons, and they're jumbled around the application window. When you choose *Arrange Icons*, Windows arranges the icons in neat rows along the bottom of the window. This command is particularly useful if you resize a window so you no longer see all the icons; they snap back into view when you choose it.

Program Manager is one Windows program that uses document windows—each program group in Program Manager is a separate document window. When you first start Program Manager, all the program groups are reduced to icons so you see them in rows along the bottom of the window. (Click on the Program Manager Window, if necessary, to display it.) Try opening several to get experience working with multiple document windows:

1. Double-click on these program groups to open their windows: Main, Accessories, and StartUp. (You may have to drag open document windows away from the bottom of the Program Manager window so you can click on program icons.)

The document windows appear within the Program Manager window, overlapped one over the other.

2. Choose *Tile* from the Window menu.

The document windows are resized and laid out so they don't overlap.

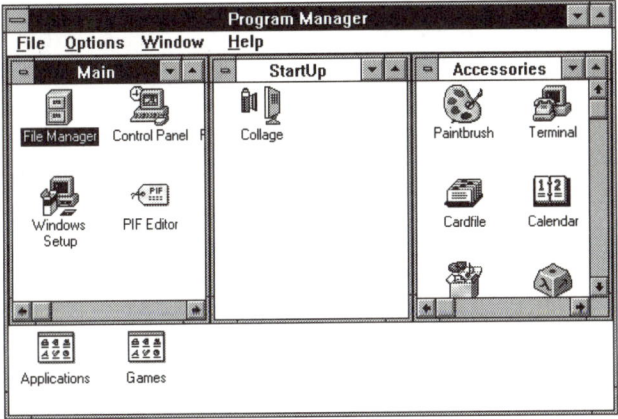

3. Choose *Cascade* from the Window menu.

The document windows are resized and overlapped in a cascade so you can see the edges of each window.

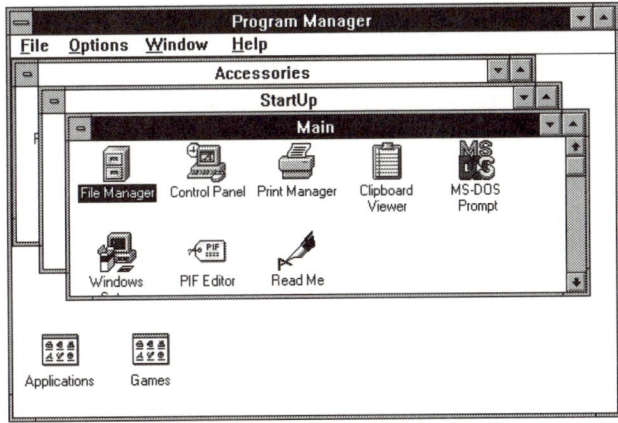

4. Double-click the control-menu box of each document window to close it.

5. Drag the group icons around in the Program Manager window so they're disorganized.

6. Choose *Arrange Icons* from Window menu.

   The icons are lined up in neat rows in the bottom of the Program Manager window.

# Getting Help

Even with standard Windows controls, it often takes some time to learn individual Windows programs; each program has its own unique features that require unique controls. If the features don't make immediate sense to you, then you can read about them by using Windows' on-line manual (called *Help*), which appears in its own window to list individual features and explain how to use each one.

## Using the Help Window

Start Help by choosing a command from the Help menu in the application window where you're stumped. The contents of the Help menu can vary from window to window. Some programs offer Help commands that run you through tutorials, others offer only rudimentary help. One command that you should find in every Help menu is *Contents* (sometimes called *Help Index*). Choosing *Contents* opens the Help window (shown in Figure 4-12), where you can search for the information you need.

The Help window displays information in separate topics. You might think of each topic as an information card; it displays information about a single subject. If the information in a topic is lengthy, you can scroll through it with the vertical scroll bar on the side of the Help window.

Sprinkled throughout the text of a topic are *hot spots,* which stand out from the text around them because they're underlined and are set in color. Whenever you click on a hot spot, you display new information. If you click on a *definition* (a hot spot underlined with a dotted line), you open a small window with a definition of the word that's underlined. (Click anywhere with the mouse or press any key on the keyboard to close the definition window.) If you click on a *topic title* (a hot spot underlined with a solid line), you jump to a new topic in the Help window.

Control buttons ————

Definition ————

Topic title ————

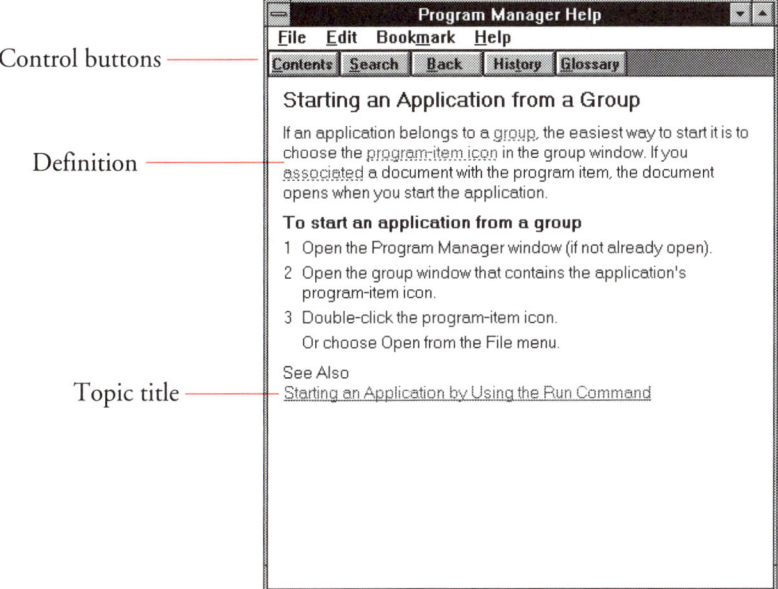

*Figure 4-12* The Help window displays topics for you to read.

## So What about About?

The Help menu contains one command that doesn't have anything to do with on-line help: the About... command, which often contains the name of whatever program you're running: About Write..., About File Manager..., and so on. This command opens a window that gives you technical information about the program, such as its name, its version, and how much free memory you have left on your computer system. Use the command if you want to check on available memory before you start another program, or if you just want to know who's responsible for the software you're running.

## Moving to New Topics

You move from topic to topic in Help by clicking on topic titles that interest you. To see all the topics available in Help, read the *Contents topic,* a topic which lists the titles of all other topics. Help displays the Contents topic when you first open the Help window. Whenever you want to see the Contents topic, you click on the Contents button at the top of the Help window; you'll return to the Contents topic from whatever topic you were reading.

Most topics include embedded topic titles that lead to related information, which should help you find the information you need in the order you need it. For example, you may go to a topic called "Saving documents." As you read, you find a topic titled "The Save command," which gives you more specific information about the Save command. Chaining through topics this way often shows you information about features you didn't know existed in a program.

Try reading help for the Program Manager:

1.  Choose *Contents* from the Help menu in order to open the Help window.

2.  Click on the topic title *Arrange Windows and Icons.*

    The Help window displays a topic explaining how to arrange windows and icons.

3.  Click on the definition *title bar* (which is underlined with a dotted line).

    A definition box opens, defining the term "title bar."

    > **title bar**
    >
    > The horizontal bar at the top of a window that contains the title of the window or dialog box. On many windows, the title bar also contains the Control-menu box and Maximize and Minimize buttons.

4.  Click anywhere to close the definition box.

5.  Double-click on the Contents button to return to the Contents topic.

## Finding Your Way around Topics

If you get lost as you chain your way through Help topics, you can always return to the Contents topic by clicking on the Contents button. To methodically work your way back through your chain of topics, click on the Back button; each click takes you one step further back along the chain of topics you've already read through. To jump back several topics at one step, click on the History button, which opens the History window shown in Figure 4-13. You'll see a list there of the topics you've read through; double-click on the one you want, to close the History window and see your topic in the Help window.

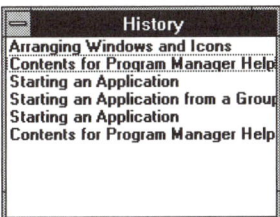

*Figure 4-13* The History window lists, in order, the topics you've read through in the Help window.

Many times topic titles don't tell you where you need to find a specific piece of information. If so, you can use the Search option, which you start by clicking on the Search button at the top of the Help window. It opens the Search window (shown in Figure 4-14). The Search window shows a list of subjects in the list at the top of the window, which you can think of as an alphabetically organized index. Scroll through it to find the subject you're looking for, then double-click on the subject when you find it.

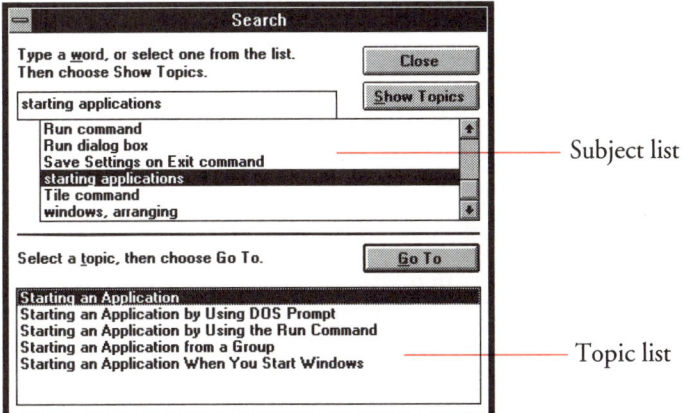

*Figure 4-14* The Search window offers an index of subjects explained in help, and shows the topics where you can find information for each subject.

The topic list in the bottom of the Search window shows the title of every available topic that contains information about your selected subject. To read one of those topics, double-click on it. The Search window closes, and the Help window displays the topic you asked for.

Try searching for a subject in the Help window:

1. Click on the Search button to open the Search window.

2. Scroll through the Subjects list until you see the subject *starting applications* (or a similar title).

3. Double-click on *starting applications.*

   Five different topics with information about starting applications appear in the Topics list.

4. Double-click on the topic *Starting an Application from a Group.*

   The Search window closes, and the topic *Starting an Application from a Group* appears in the Help window.

5. Quit Help by double-clicking on its control-menu box.

---

### I Hate Looking up the Same Topic Again and Again!

There are some things that just don't stick in the memory —an obscure (but useful) technique or a complicated set of steps, perhaps. If you find yourself looking up the same topic over and over, print it out so you can pin it up within sight and refer to it instantly. First find your frustrating topic in the Help window, then choose *Print Topic* from the File menu. If your printer is turned on and ready to print, Help prints the topic on paper for your convenience.

In the File menu, you'll also find a Printer Setup command which you can use to set a different printer (if you have more than one connected to your computer) or if you need to set the kind of paper you're going to print on. If you've never set up a printer before, you'll find more information about it in Chapter 8.

# Quitting an Application

Whenever you're finished working in a program, you can quit the program in any one of several ways, depending on which is most convenient for you:

- Choose *Exit* from the File menu
- Choose *Close* from the control menu
- Double-click the control-menu button in the upper-left corner of the application window

When you quit using any of these methods, most programs don't just shut down and leave the desktop, because they don't want to wipe out any unsaved work you might have still open in the application window. To make sure you want to quit, they put up an exit message that tells you that you have unsaved work. It offers to save your work you several command buttons:

- **Save (or Yes)** Saves your document (using a Save As dialog box if the document is unnamed) and then closes the application

- **No** Immediately closes the application, erasing any unsaved work

- **Cancel** Cancels your request to quit, returning you to the program as it was

Decide what you want to do, then click on the button you want. This is one step where you *don't* want to get into automatic habits. If you automatically click on *Save (or Yes),* you may find yourself saving a revised version of a document that erases an original version you wanted to keep. If you automatically click on *No,* you may lose work that you forgot to save. And if you automatically click on *Cancel,* you'll never quit the program, and will be forced to keep working until they pry your twitching fingers from the keyboard!

You've now made your way through the standard features of a Windows program. You should feel more at home when you start a strange application, so this is a good time to go exploring. Try starting some of Windows accessory programs such as Draw or Write, then look through the menus and onscreen controls to see what you can do with them. If you get stumped with custom features, you can always look through Help topics, easily quit the program with no loss of honor or, if you're really interested, read the Windows manual to find out more about each application. Have fun!

# CHAPTER

## 5

---

# MANAGING PROGRAMS

If your work in Windows is simple—say, for example, that you use only one or two standard Windows programs—then you already know all you need to know about managing programs: You find the program you want in Program Manager; then you double-click the program's icon to start the program. Simple enough.

It's in the nature of computers, however, that you'll want to do more and more, and things will get just a *little* more complex. You may find some great new programs and install them on your computer. How do you make sure they appear in Program Manager? You may have programs that don't run under Windows and need a DOS command to start. Can you use Program Manager to start them without quitting Windows? Or you may just find that Program Manager is getting unbearably cluttered with programs and program groups. How can you rearrange everything in a logical order so programs are easy to find? This chapter shows you how to make Program Manager do what you want it to.

## Understanding Program Manager

Program Manager's name implies that it manages every program running under Windows; that it cracks the whip over each program to make sure that it uses the correct user interface and follows all the proper Windows rules. The name is misleading, though, because Windows does all this without Program Manager. Program Manager plays the more humble role of presenting programs for you to start. Once started, you and the program are on your own.

To best understand how Program Manager works, think of it as a program attendant—something like the head attendant at a large valet parking ramp for autos. When you want a car, you ask the parking attendant to bring it down to you, where you take the controls and drive away. When you want a program, you ask Program Manager for the program by clicking on the program's icon. Program Manager finds the program on a disk drive and starts the program; you take it from there. Program Manager then waits humbly in the background for your next request to start a program.

## Program Items

Each of the program icons you click on in Program Manager is a *program item.* Although it's tempting to think that a program item is the program itself (I click on it and the program starts! What more evidence do you need?), it's not. It's simply a small file that stores a DOS command for starting a program. When you double-click on a program item, Program Manager reads the program item file and then executes the DOS command there. This starts the program from a program file that may be stored anywhere on the computer system.

Think of a program item as a key hook in the parking attendant's office. You point to the hook labeled "1969 brown Ford Fairlane," and the attendant takes the key hung there and goes to fetch the car from the ramp. You don't need to know where the car is parked, only where the key is hung in the office. In the same way, when you double-click on a program item, you simply let Program Manager know what program you want. You don't need to know where the program actually resides on disk.

A program item file actually stores a little more information than just a DOS command. It also stores the item's name (which may be different than the program's real name), the picture used for the item's icon, and minor details about how the program should run once started. Most of this information is just item labeling, in the way that the key hook in the last example could show a picture of your Fairlane, have the label "Brown Bomb" (even though that's not the official car name), and contain a note that you want the car warmed up thoroughly before you take it out.

## Program Groups

To help you make sense of large numbers of program items, Program Manager groups items together in *program groups.* They function somewhat like directories do in File Manager—they organize programs (if you're tidy) in a logical and efficient way. Program groups are simpler than directories, however. To begin with, you can't have program groups inside of other program groups, so what you see in the Program Manager window is what you get—no hidden program groups. In addition, program items must always be stored within a program group, so you won't see program items mixed in with program groups in the Program Manager window. These restrictions help keep Program Manager uncluttered and simple to use.

Just as program item information is stored in a program item file, program group information is stored in a program group file. The file contains the name and icon picture of the program group, and the name of each program item contained in the group. Whenever you double-click on a program group to open it, Program Manager reads the program group file so that it knows what program items to show inside the program group window. If you want to change the program group, you can change its file to set its contents, name, and appearance.

## Working with Program Groups

When you first install and run Windows, the Installer automatically creates five program groups in Program Manager:

- **Main**    Stores Windows' main programs, such as File Manager and Print Manager

- **Accessories**    Stores other applications that come with Windows, such as Notepad and Paint

- **Games**    Stores Windows game programs, such as Solitaire and Minesweeper

- **StartUp**    Stores any programs that you want to start automatically as soon as you start Windows

- **Applications**    Stores other application programs that Windows found on your hard disk when Windows was installed

If you install a new program, it may automatically create its own program group and program items during installation. For example, if you install Microsoft Word for Windows, its installation program creates a Word for Windows program group with a Word for Windows program item inside it.

If every program you install on your computer creates its own program group and program items and if you like their organization, then you need fiddle no further with program groups. If, on the other hand, you want to organize according to your own principles (why have a separate Word for Windows group anyway, you might ask), it's a simple matter to create your own program groups.

## Creating a Program Group

To create a new program group, you ask Program Manager for a new group, and then give it a name. Try it now to create a program group named "Workhorses I Use," where you can store all the programs you use the most:

1. If you haven't started Windows yet, turn your computer on and start Windows.

2. If you see any open program group windows in Program Manager, close them so that you see only icons in the Program Manager window.

3. Choose *New* from the File menu.

   A dialog box opens where you can choose between creating a new program item or a new program group.

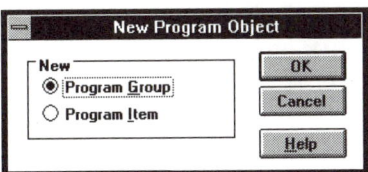

4. If necessary, click the Program Group button to select it.

5. Click the OK button.

   The dialog box closes, and a new dialog box opens where you can give your program group a name.

6. Click in the Description text area and type `Workhorses I Use`, then click the OK button.

   The dialog box closes and a new (and empty) program group window labeled *Workhorses I Use* appears in the Program Manager window.

7. Click the minimize button in the Workhorses window to reduce it to a program group icon.

You've now created a new program group, which you named "Workhorses I Use." When you filled in the program group name, you probably noticed a second text area in the dialog box that asked for the group file. This was a place to give the program group file a name, but you didn't need to fill anything in. When you leave it blank, Windows takes the first eight characters of the group name, adds the file extension ".GRP", and saves the information for your new program group under that file name. The program group you just created is stored in the program group file workhors.grp.

## Changing the Name of a Program Group

If you'd like to change the name of a program group, use the Properties command in the File menu. Try it now to reduce the clunky name "Workhorses I Use" to something more manageable:

1. If necessary, click on the Workhorses I Use icon to select it.

2. Choose *Properties* from the File menu.

   A dialog box opens showing you the current name and program group file name for the program group.

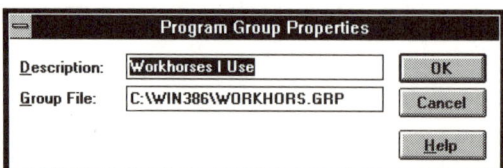

3. Click at the end of the name in the Description text area, use Backspace to reduce the name to *Workhorses*, then click the OK button to close the dialog box.

   The program group name now reads *Workhorses*.

Notice that you could also have changed the group file name; it's best to leave that alone unless you have some tricky group file chicanery in mind, an activity for advanced Windows users only.

### Deleting a Program Group

To delete a program group from the window, you select it and then choose *Delete* from the File menu. Any program items in the program group are deleted with the group. Don't worry, though, no programs are actually erased when you delete a program group, just the program group and program item files that point to those programs. You can restore program items to Program Manager, as you'll see later in this chapter.

## Working with Program Items

Once you have the program groups you want in Program Manager, you can fill them with the program items you want in each group. You can move a program item from one group to another; you can delete program items that you never use; you can rename program items; you can even create more than one program item for the same program.

### Moving Program Items

To move a program item from one program group to another, you open up the program group where the item is located and then drag the item from that group to the second group. You can drop the item into the second group's window if it's open, or directly on the group icon if the window is closed. (For now, close the Workhorses group.) Try it now to move the Write application to your Workhorse group:

1. Double-click the group icon Accessories to open the Accessories program group.

2. If the Accessories window covers up the other group icons, drag the window far enough out of the way so you can see the icons.

3. Find the program item Write in the Accessories window, drag the item icon out of the window until it's directly over the Workhorses group icon.

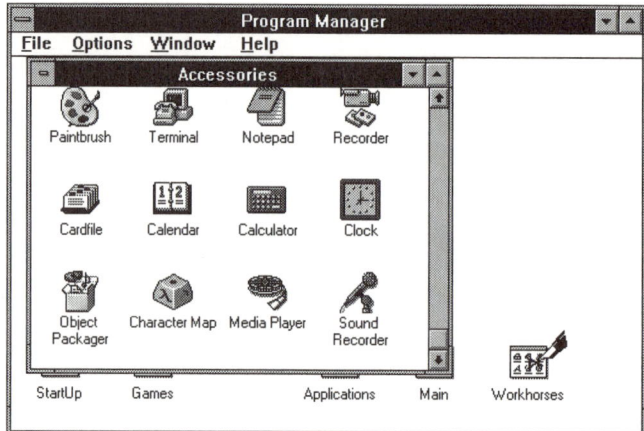

4. Drop the icon by releasing the mouse button.

   Write is no longer in the Accessories program group.

5. Double-click the Workhorses group icon to open the program group.

   Write appears in the Workhorses program group.

6. Close all program group windows so you see only program group icons.

## Copying Program Items

If you'd like, you can copy a program item so the item appears in two groups at the same time. This can be a good way to resolve a conflict over which group to place the item—just put it in both! For example, you may want a word processor program item to appear in a Words program group (filled with word-processing-related programs) and also in the Applications program group, where you expect to find every application available to you.

To copy an item, you drag just as you did to move an item, but you hold down the Ctrl key as you drag. Try copying the Solitaire program item from the Games program group into the Workhorses program group so you can play solitaire from either group:

1.  Open the Games program group and move its window (if necessary) so you can see the Workhorses group icon at the same time.

2.  Hold down the Ctrl key on the keyboard, then drag the Solitaire program item from the Games window and drop it on the Workhorses group icon.

    The Solitaire item remains in the Games window.

3.  Open the Workhorses program group. You see the Solitaire program item in the Workhorses window, where you can start it if you wish.

## Deleting a Program Item

To delete a program item, you simply select its icon and then use the Delete command in the File menu. Try it now to remove the all-too-distracting Solitaire from your Workhorses program group:

1.  Click on the Solitaire item in the Workhorses window to select Solitaire.

2.  Choose *Delete* from the File menu.

    A dialog box appears that asks you if you really want to go through with it.

3.  Resolutely click the Yes button.

    The dialog box disappears and Solitaire is removed from the Workhorses program group.

4.  Close all program group windows so you see only icons in Program Manager.

Remember that deleting a program item doesn't delete the program itself from your computer, it only removes the program item file. If you want to restore the item, you can recreate it as a new item.

## Creating a Program Item

There will come a time when you have a program you want to start in Program Manager, but the program has no program item. Maybe you've accidentally deleted the item or you bought a program that doesn't automatically create an item when you install the program on your computer. If so, you can easily add a program item, using the New command in the File menu.

Try restoring the Solitaire program item you deleted earlier by creating a new Solitaire program item:

1. Double-click on the Workhorses icon to open it and select it as the program group where you want to add a program item.

2. Choose *New* from the File menu to open the New Program Object dialog box.

3. If necessary, click the Program Item button, then click the OK button.

   The dialog box closes, and the Program Item Properties dialog box opens.

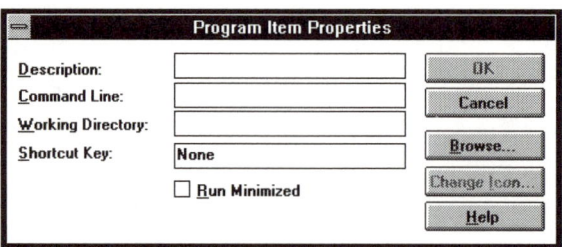

4. Enter `Solitaire` in the Description text area. (This sets the name of your new program item.)

5. Click the Browse button to locate the program file you want.

   The Browse dialog box opens; it looks and works almost exactly like a standard Open dialog box.

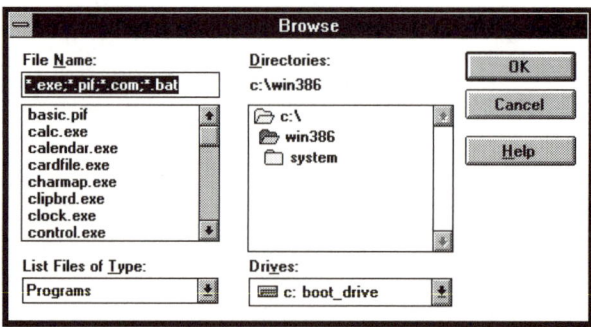

## I Want to Start a Program with a Document Already Open

You may be a person who likes to start your work with the same document every time. For example, you might always go straight to your to-do list when you start your word processor, or to your daily balance sheet when you start your spreadsheet program. If so, you can set up a program item in Program Manager that automatically starts the program with that document. It's a simple trick:

When you browse through your hard disk for a program to enter in the Command Line text area of the Program Item Properties dialog box, select *.* from the File Type box so that you see all the files available in each directory. Then double-click on a document name instead of a program name. When Windows creates a program item using the document, it knows what program created the document and uses its icon for the program item. For example, if you create a program item for a Write document file named "todolist.wri," you'll see a program item that uses Write's pen-tip icon.

When you double-click on a document program item, you start the program with the document open. For example, double-clicking on the to-do list item starts Write with your to-do list open so you can look at it right away.

6. Scroll through the files in the file name list until you find the file name *sol.exe*, then double-click on it. (This file is located in the Windows or Win386 directory.)

   The dialog box closes, and the full pathname for sol.exe appears in the Command Line text area.

7. Click the OK button.

   The dialog box closes, and the new item *Solitaire* appears in the window.

8. Close the Workhorses window so you can see the other program group icons.

When you create a new program item this way, you give it a name with the text you enter in the Description text area. When you browse through program files and choose a program for the item, you put the program's full pathname in the Command Line text area. This pathname is an MS-DOS command that Program Manager executes to start the program you want. Note that you can choose an MS-DOS program as well as a Windows program to start when you double-click the item. This allows you to set up in Program Manager a program item that starts an MS-DOS program.

## Editing a Program Item

If you'd like to rename a program item or change any of its other properties, you first select the item and then choose *Properties* from the File menu. This reopens the Program Item Properties dialog box where you can see the item's current properties and change them if you wish.

You already know what the Description, Command Line, and Browse controls do. The other controls are:

- **Working Directory**   Sets the directory where your program normally saves documents. This is usually the same directory where the program file is stored. If you want a different working directory, enter its full pathname here. (Keep in mind that you can always override the working directory by specifying a different directory when you save a document.)

- **Shortcut Key**   Sets a key combination to activate the program when it's running at the same time as other programs. To set the combination, click in the text area and then press any keyboard key you want to use. (The next chapter gives you more information about this feature.)

- **Run Minimized**    When turned on (with an "x" in its check-box), sets the program to start as an icon instead of as a fully opened window. This is a useful option if you want the program to wait in the background once you start it for the time when you need it.
- **Change Icon**    Lets you choose the icon you see in the program group window. When you click on this button, a dialog box opens with a scroll bar that lets you look at the available icons, something like paging through a book of mug shots (but only if the program offers more than one icon). Click on the icon you want, then click *OK* to select the icon.

# Keeping Program Manager Neat

You can arrange Program Manager as you do a desk: casually, with stacks of open windows and jumbled icons scattered throughout; or neatly, with orderly open windows and rows of icons. If you like to keep things neat, Program Manager offers several helpful commands in the Window menu. You learned about two of them in the last chapter: Cascade and Tile, which arrange open program group windows in a cascade or tiled arrangement. A third command, *Arrange Icons,* helps keep icons arranged in neat rows within a window. We touched on it briefly before.

Before you choose *Arrange Icons,* click on the Program Manager window where you want to clean up the icons. If it's a program group window, be sure it's open and on top of other program group windows. If it's the Program Manager window itself, make sure all program group windows are reduced to icons. When you choose *Arrange Icons,* Program Manager fits all the icons to the window's current size, lining them up in neat rows along the bottom of the window.

Try using Arrange Icons on the Accessories program group:

1. Double-click the Accessories icon to open its window.

2. Resize the Accessories window so that it's tall and narrow.

    The icons in the window disappear off one side of the window.

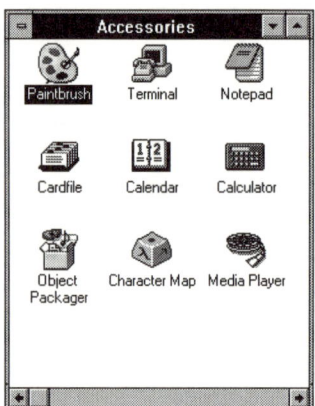

3. Choose *Arrange Icons* from the Window menu.

    The icons rearrange themselves to fit in orderly rows within the window. If the window size is too small to accommodate all the icons, the extra icons are positioned off the bottom of the window.

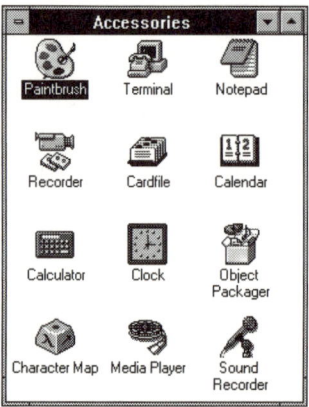

4. Close the Accessories window.

Arrange Icons is very useful after you resize a window, because it rearranges icons to fit the new window size. If you find that you use this command often, choose *Auto Arrange* in the Options menu to turn on auto arranging. When it's on, Program Manager automatically arranges the icons in a program group window every time you resize the window. Unfortunately, this feature works only with icons within program group windows. When you resize the Program Manager window itself, Auto Arrange won't rearrange the program group icons.

# Starting Programs

Once your program items and program groups are set up the way you like them, starting a program is a simple matter of double-clicking on a program item. If the program is a Windows program, it opens its own window (or puts up an icon if you set it to start minimized). If the program is an MS-DOS program that isn't designed to run under Windows (usually marked with an icon that reads *MS-DOS*), Windows goes away, and the MS-DOS program controls the screen. You won't see any windows, and you'll have to follow the program's own conventions. When you quit the program, Windows returns.

---

### I Want to Start an MS-DOS Program from MS-DOS

If you want to start an MS-DOS program that has no program item in Program Manager, you don't have to quit Windows to get back to MS-DOS. Go instead to the Main program group, where you'll find an icon labeled *MS-DOS Prompt*. When you double-click this icon, Windows switches to an MS-DOS screen where you can enter standard MS-DOS commands. You can start your program here. When you're finished and want to return to Windows, simply enter `exit` at the prompt; the MS-DOS screen disappears, and Windows returns.

---

## Getting the Program Manager Window out of the Way

If, when you run a Windows program from Program Manager and find that the Program Manager window clutters up the screen, you can turn on *Minimize on Use* in the Options menu. When it's on, Program Manager minimizes itself to an icon whenever you start a program, so that Program Manager is out of the way while you work. When you quit your program, you can restore Program Manager by double-clicking on its icon.

## Setting a Program to Start When You Start Windows

You may have a program that you always start immediately as soon as you start Windows. If you'd like to save yourself some time, you can set up that program as a *startup program,* a program that Windows runs when you first start Windows, so that the program is ready and waiting for you.

To set up a startup program, simply move or copy the program's icon into the StartUp program group in Program Manager. Windows automatically starts any programs it finds there when you first run Windows. You can, if you like, put many different programs in here, but to avoid clutter, you should set some of them to minimize when run so that you see only the program icon instead of the program's fully open window.

# Quitting Program Manager

Whenever you quit Program Manager, you quit Windows as well. And when you quit Windows, it normally takes a "snapshot" of the way Program Manager is laid out—the arrangement of windows and icons—and saves that arrangement to disk so that it can restore the same arrangement when you restart Windows later. This means that if you quit with a cluttered Program Manager window, you'll see the same clutter when you come back the next day.

The Save Settings on Exit option in the Options menu controls this exiting snapshot. As long as the option is turned on (which it usually is), Windows takes the snapshot. If the option is turned off, then Windows won't take the snapshot, and Program Manager will start each session with the same arrangement.

If you've got everything in Program Manager arranged exactly the way you like it and you want to start every Windows session that way, save your settings and then make sure you don't save them again: Turn on *Save Settings on Exit* if it's not turned on. Quit Windows by quitting Program Manager so that Windows will save your Program Manager arrangement to disk, then restart Windows. Now turn off the Save Settings on Exit option and leave it off. Turn it on again only when you want to save a new Program Manager arrangement.

Before you quit Program Manager for real, take a few moments to get rid of the sample program group you created in this chapter's examples:

1. Double-click on the Workhorses program group to open it.
2. Drag the program item Write from the Workhorses window back to the Accessories program group where you found it originally.
3. Click on the Workhorses window to select it.
4. Choose *Delete* from the File menu.
5. When Windows asks if you're sure you want to delete the group, click the Yes button.

   The Workhorses group disappears from Program Manager.

Now that you know some of the intricacies of Program Manager, you can customize it with the program items and program groups you want, and you can arrange it to make it comfortable for your style of working. In the next chapter, you see how to handle all the programs you can start with Program Manager.

# CHAPTER
# 6

---

# RUNNING SEVERAL PROGRAMS AT ONCE

One of Windows' best features is its ability to run more than one program at a time. You can move from one program to another like a cook in a busy kitchen, concentrating on one project while other projects simmer in the background. The trick, as in any successful kitchen, is to know where to focus your attention and how to move ingredients successfully from pot to pot. And as you work, you must be able to keep the counter clean so you can see what you're doing.

As you read through this chapter, you see how to successfully cook with several programs running at once in Windows. You're introduced to Task List, a convenient tool for organizing your running programs, and to the clipboard, which helps you transfer ingredients from program to program. You're also introduced to some interesting concepts with clunky names: *multitasking* and *embedded objects*.

# How Windows Runs Several Programs at Once

Whenever you use Program Manager to start a program, you run at least two programs at one time: Program Manager and the program you started. You can, of course, start more programs as well; Windows keeps the program activities in separate windows. If you go from one program to another by moving to a new application window, the program left behind may sit idly in its window—the way a word processor waits for more text from you—or the program may work on its own in the background. Windows' Print Manager, for example, can print a document on the printer while you work in a different program.

Windows' ability to allow two or more programs to work simultaneously is called *multitasking*. Think of multitasking as the computer's ability to do what you do naturally as you walk down the street and simultaneously whistle a tune.

## Understanding Multitasking

A computer isn't naturally inclined to multitasking; it's a machine that drudgingly executes one instruction at a time in a straight line, and it hates to be diverted. If you run your computer under MS-DOS alone, you find this to be true: You must quit one application before working with another. So how does Windows allow you to run several programs at once? It takes advantage of the computer's tremendous speed.

Imagine the computer as a single—but very fast—teller in a bank with a line of teller windows. When a single customer comes up to a window, the teller spends all his time on the customer's transaction, waiting while the customer fills out deposit slips and endorses checks. When a second customer comes in, the teller has some spare time to sneak over to the second customer while the first customer fills out forms. Because the teller is so much faster than the customers, he can move back and forth between the two windows and take up each customer's request at the instant they're made. It appears to each customer that the teller is working exclusively with them.

This is the essence of multitasking. The computer moves quickly from one active program to another, working a little in each program so that each program appears to be running on its own. Multitasking works as well as it does because the computer executes its tasks much more quickly than we execute ours; it has plenty of time between our plodding keystrokes and mouse clicks to sort records in a data base or send information to a printer.

Because all running Windows programs are served by a single multitasking computer, arduous work in one program can slow down the other programs with it. Consider a customer in the bank asking the teller to count a huge pile of pennies. The teller sneaks away now and then to attend to the other customers, but because he's so busy with the pennies, those visits are rare; all customers get slow service. In the same way, if you ask a spreadsheet to perform intensive calculations in the background, other running programs suddenly work much more slowly, to the point where typing and even mouse clicks seem sluggish in the program where you're working.

Running many programs at once in Windows is another way to slow down overall performance, just as a teller serving twenty customers isn't nearly as fast as a teller serving only three customers. If you run enough programs at once, you'll see slower performance even if the programs in the background aren't hard at work.

## Operating Modes

Some computers can bring more powerful features to bear on multitasking; they make multitasking work with greater speed and efficiency. To take advantage of these features, Windows can operate in either one of two modes: Enhanced or Standard. If you have a computer with a powerful 80386 or 80486 processor supported with sufficient memory, Windows runs in Enhanced mode, which allows you to run more programs at one time than you can in Standard mode. Enhanced mode also offers control over which running program receives the most of the computer's attention.

Computers with less powerful processors or limited memory run Windows in Standard mode, which doesn't support as many programs running at one time. Standard mode doesn't offer the same control of multitasking efficiency that you can find in Enhanced mode.

If you don't know whether your computer is running Windows in Standard or Enhanced mode, choose *About Program Manager* from the Help menu in the Program Manager window. The dialog box that opens (Figure 6-1) shows the mode in the bottom of the box.

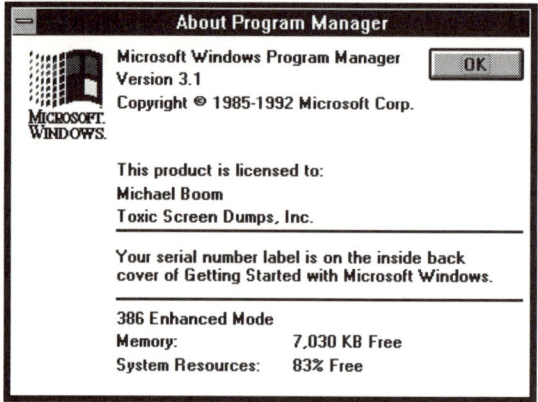

*Figure 6-1* The About Program Manager dialog box shows you in which mode you're running Windows.

## How Can I Speed Things up When I Run Several Programs at Once?

If you're the type of Windows user who never quits a program, you may find that Windows gets cluttered with application windows and that your applications start to run appreciably slower. How can you speed things up so you don't have to twiddle your thumbs but still have your applications available in an instant?

The simplest solution is to quit programs that you aren't going to use for a while. This frees up computer memory, clears up your workspace, and gives your computer more processing time to devote to the programs you are using. But it doesn't leave your programs on the desktop for instant access.

Another simple solution—if you have some extra money that you don't mind spending—is to upgrade your computer system by adding more memory or by getting a computer with a faster processor. The extra memory speeds up performance because your computer has more memory to devote to each program and won't have to juggle memory among competing programs as often. The faster processor speeds up performance through brute force, executing instructions at a quicker rate—the equivalent of hiring a faster teller in a bank.

Finally, if you're technically inclined and don't mind wading through esoterica in the Windows manual, you can twiddle with performance settings for your computer. Particularly handy for Enhanced mode Windows users is the 386 Enhanced control in Windows' Control Panel. You can use it to set Windows to devote more time to your active program and less time to programs running in the background.

# Keeping Order among Programs

It's easy to start many programs at once in Windows: you simply double-click program icons in Program Manager until Windows informs you that it doesn't have enough memory to run more programs. Keeping order among all those programs is another matter. Fortunately, Windows offers some convenient tools for keeping a tidy desktop and for finding the program you want when you need it. To use those tools, you should understand the concept of active and background programs.

## Active and Background Programs

When you work with several programs at once, Windows sees to it that only one of those programs is the *active program*, the program where you're working. You can recognize the active program: the title of its window or its icon is highlighted, and its window or icon rests on top of every other window and icon on the desktop. All other running programs are *background programs*.

The active program is the only program that accepts your keystrokes and mouse actions—an important distinction, because if Windows allowed more than one active window at a time, you wouldn't know where your typing or mouse work would go. The background programs (misleadingly called "inactive programs" in the Windows documentation and screens) don't accept your input, but they can work in the background.

Because a working background program might come across a problem of some kind that needs your resolution (a program runs out of memory while calculating, for example), Windows notifies you when a background program has a message: it beeps and flashes the title bar or icon of the working program. When you see or hear the alert, switch to that program to read the message in its window.

## Switching from Program to Program

You already know one method of switching from program to program: you click a program's window or icon, and it becomes the active program. There's one drawback to this technique, though. You have to see a window or icon before you can click it. If other windows cover the program you want, you have to move, resize, or minimize windows until you see the program. To make life simpler, Windows offers alternative techniques for switching from program to program.

## Pressing Alt+Tab

Whenever you hold down the Alt key and press Tab, Windows presents you with the name of a running program. By pressing Tab repeatedly, you cycle through the names of all running programs until you get to the program you want. You then release the Alt key, and Windows brings the program's window to the top as the active program. Try it now:

1. Turn on your computer and run Windows, if it isn't already running.

2. Start Notepad, Write, and Paintbrush. All three programs should be in the Accessories program group. You may have to move windows around to get back to Program Manager each time to start a new program.

The desktop fills with windows for Program Manager, Notepad, Write, and Paintbrush. The last program you started is the active window, located on top of all the other windows.

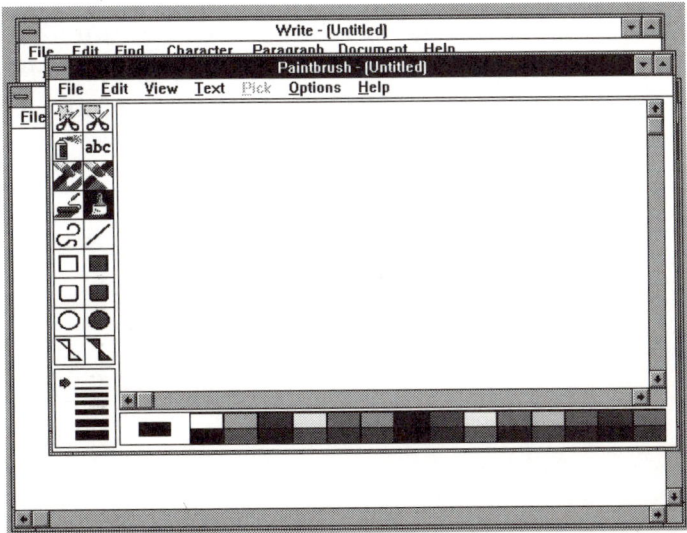

3. Hold down the Alt key.

4. Tap the Tab key.

Windows presents the name of a program in the middle of the desktop.

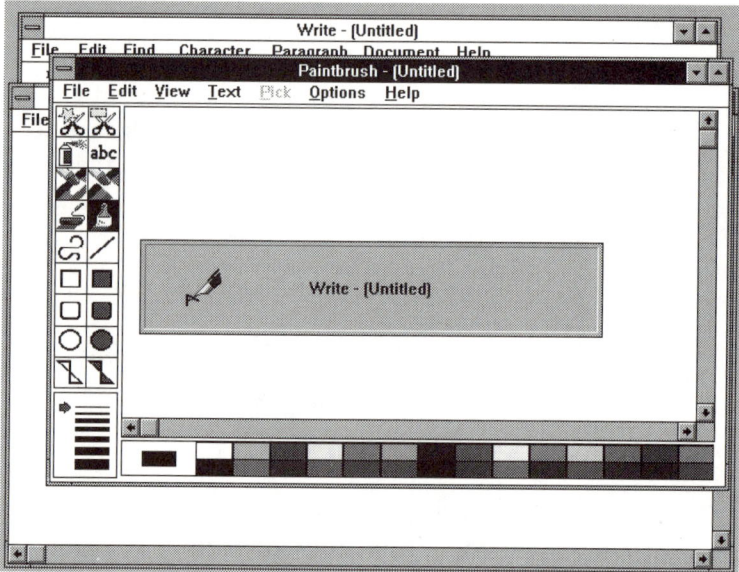

5. Still holding down the Alt key, continue to tap the Tab key until you read the program name *Program Manager*.

Windows presents the names of different running programs until it reaches *Program Manager*.

6. Release the Alt key.

Windows makes Program Manager the active program, putting its window on top of all others.

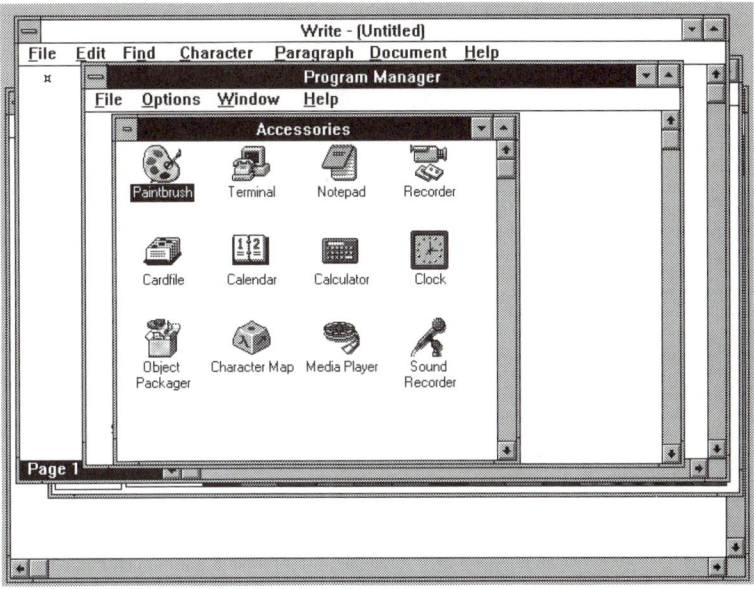

## Task List

Task List (shown in Figure 6-2) provides another quick way to switch programs. To open Task List, double-click any part of the desktop not covered by a window or icon, or choose *Switch To* from the control menu of any application window.

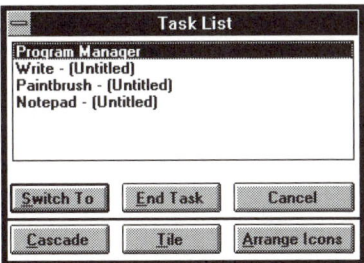

*Figure 6-2* Task List provides a list of running programs from which you can choose; it also provides application window management tools.

With Task List open, simply double-click the name of any program listed there to switch to that program. Task List closes and that program's window becomes the active window. Try it out:

1. Choose *Switch To* from Program Manager's control menu.

   Task List opens.

2. Double-click *Notepad* in Task List.

   Task List closes, and the Notepad window comes to the top as the active window.

## Organizing Windows and Icons

If you want to switch from program to program by simply clicking on the window or icon you want, you need to keep the desktop orderly. You already know one technique for uncluttering the desktop: you can minimize an application window to an icon. The program in the window continues to work while the window is reduced to an icon, even though you can't see its progress. To return to the program, you simply double-click the icon to reopen its window.

Task List offers additional tools for ordering windows and icons on the desktop. You'll find them in three buttons at the bottom of Task List:

- **Cascade**  Sizes and overlaps application windows on the desktop like fanned playing cards.

- **Tile**  Sizes and arranges application windows so they fill the desktop without overlapping.

- **Arrange Icons**  Arranges any minimized windows on the desktop in neat rows along the bottom of the desktop.

If these commands seems familiar, they should; you use the same commands in an application window to arrange document windows and icons. Try them now:

1. Double-click the desktop's background to open Task List.

2. Click the Cascade button.

   Windows arranges the application windows so they're cascaded on the desktop.

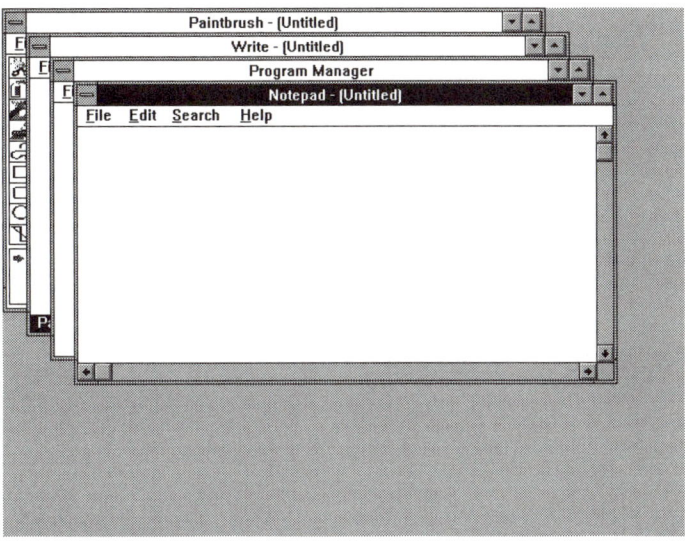

3. Repeat Step 1.

4. Click the Tile button.

Windows arranges the application windows so they're tiled on the desktop.

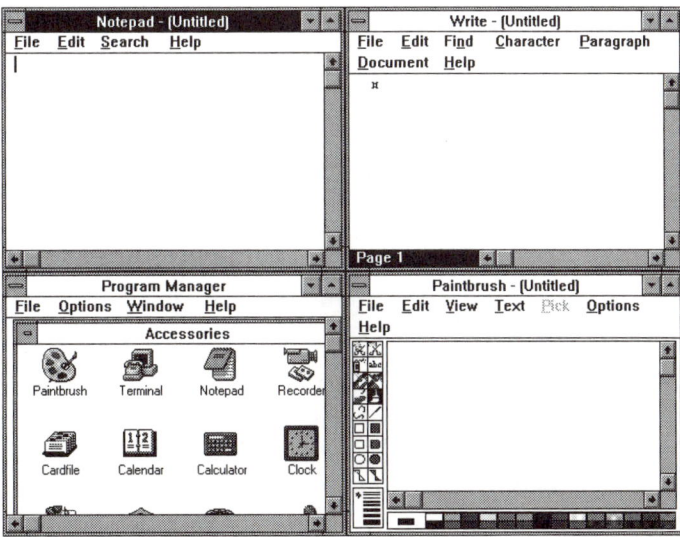

5. Repeat Step 2 to return to the cascade arrangement.

## Quitting a Running Program

If you don't want to return to a program's window or icon to quit a program, you can use Task List to quit a program. Choose the program from the list, then click the End Task button. The program quits and its window closes. Try it now to quit Notepad:

1. Click on the desktop background.

   Task List opens.

2. Click *Notepad* in the list of running programs.

3. Click the End Task button.

   Notepad quits and its window closes.

# Sharing Information among Programs

One reason it's useful to run more than one program at a time in Windows is that you can bring different programs to bear on a single project. For example, you can use Paintbrush to draw a map to a party and then use Write to type up the directions that accompany the map. Once you finish the individual components of a project, you need to assemble them all in one document, which is where the clipboard comes in.

## The Clipboard

As you learned in Chapter 4, the clipboard is memory used to store information taken from a program. That information is called a *program object* and can be a block of text from a word processor, a picture from a paint or drawing program, a table of figures from a spreadsheet, or similar information concocted in any Windows program.

To put an object in the clipboard, you must first select the object in a window and then choose either *Cut* or *Copy* from the Edit menu in that window. Cut removes the selected object from a document and puts it in the clipboard; Copy makes a copy of the selected object and puts the copy in the clipboard. Because the clipboard holds only one object at a time, it drops whatever it's holding whenever you cut or copy a new object.

To put an object from one program into another program, you cut or copy the object in the first program. (This program is called the *server* because it serves the object to another program.) You then switch to a second program (called the *client* because it receives an object from a server) and choose *Paste* from the Edit menu. The object usually appears at the insertion point location or, if there is no insertion point in the client program, at the center of the workspace.

## Handling Different Object Formats

Whenever you transfer an object between two programs, you run the risk of trying to paste an object into a program that has no idea what the object is. For example, you might try to paste a picture into the Calculator, which can't handle pictures. Fortunately, the clipboard is smart about what it contains. It tells the client program what kind of object it has inside, and if the client doesn't recognize that object type, it dims the Paste command so you can't paste the object there.

You may occasionally find that you can't paste an object into a program that seems as if it should accept the object. For example, paint programs may not be able to accept a picture from a draw program because the drawn picture is stored in a different *format* than the paint program can recognize. A format is the way an object is described; think of it as a type of language used to store an object. If a client can't understand the format of an object cut or copied from a server, it won't allow you to paste the object.

Clipboard comes to the rescue by being something of a linguist. When you cut or copy an object such as a picture into the clipboard, the clipboard stores it in as many different formats as it knows. When it offers the object to the client, chances are good that the client will recognize one of those formats and accept the object.

Try using the clipboard now; create a picture in Paintbrush (the server) and copy the picture into Write (the client):

1. Switch to Paintbrush and resize its window (if necessary) so you have enough room to create a picture.

2. Click the filled-rectangle tool (the small dark square) in the paint tool strip on the left side of the Paintbrush window to prepare to draw rectangles.

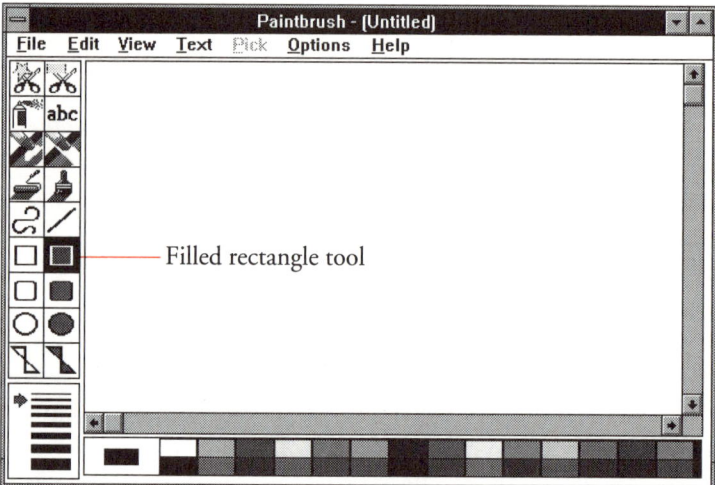

Filled rectangle tool

3. Click the red square in the strip of colors along the bottom of the window to select red as your drawing color.

4. Move the pointer into the window's workspace, drag it diagonally across a small section to create a square, then release the mouse button.

A filled red square appears where you dragged.

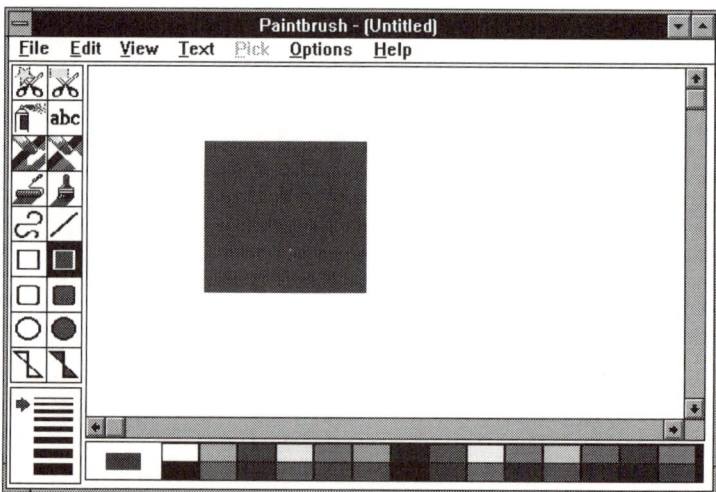

5. Click the yellow square in the color strip to select yellow as your drawing color.

6. Drag out a smaller square within the larger red square.

   A small yellow square appears within the larger red square.

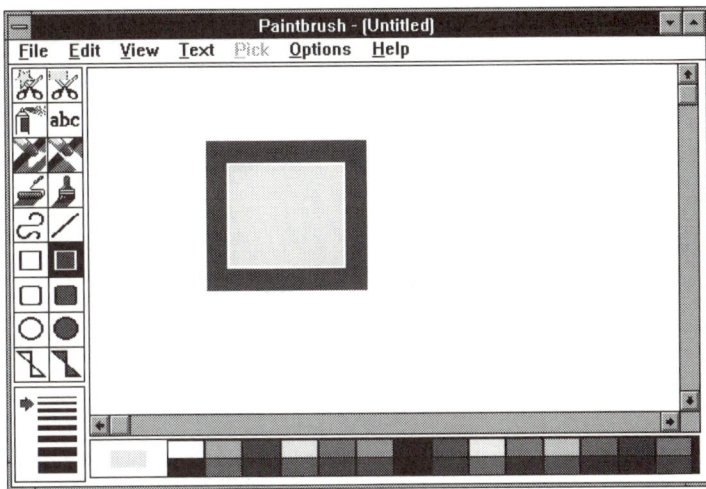

7. Click the rectangular selection tool (it includes a pair of scissors) at the top right of the tool strip to prepare to select a picture in the workspace.

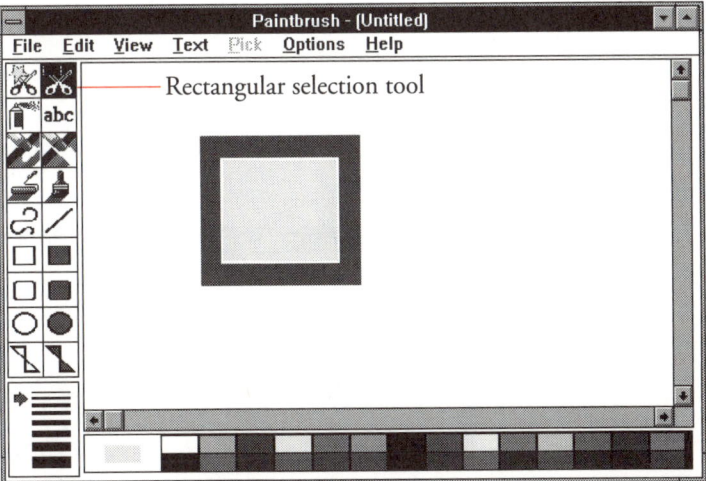

Rectangular selection tool

8. Drag from one corner of the red square to the opposite corner to put a dotted selection rectangle around the red square.

The dotted rectangle encloses the part of the workspace that you've selected; it defines the object you want to transfer to Write.

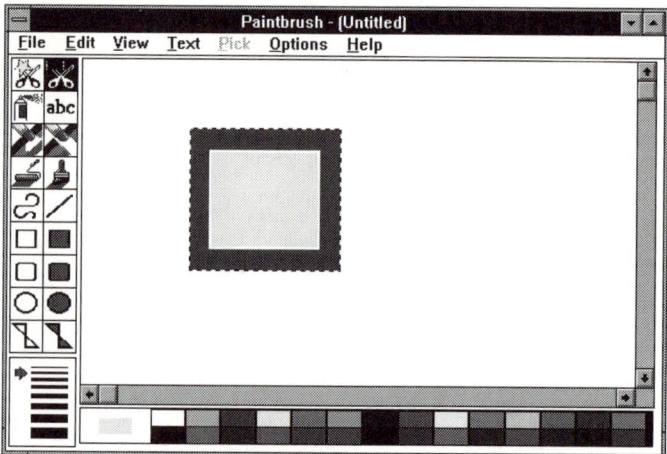

9. Choose *Copy* from the Edit menu to put a copy of your selected square into the clipboard.

10. Switch to Write and resize its window until it's large enough to work in comfortably.

11. Type `This is a picture I created in Paintbrush:` and press Enter twice.

12. Choose *Paste* from the Edit menu.

   The rectangle appears in the Write document at the insertion point location.

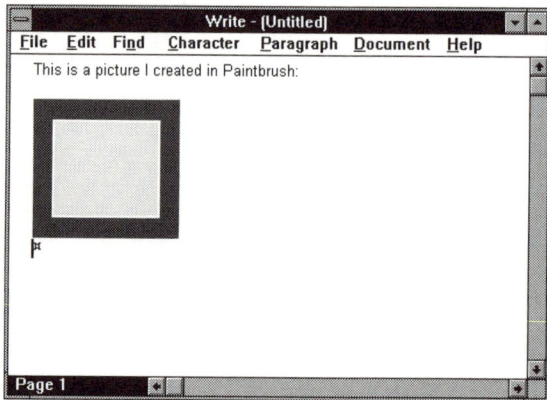

## Clipboard Viewer

If you use the clipboard often to transfer objects between programs, you may forget what you last clipped to it. To check clipboard contents, you can run a program named *Clipboard Viewer*, which you can find in the Main program group of Program Manager. It opens a window (shown in Figure 6-3) that displays the clipboard contents.

*Figure 6-3* Clipboard Viewer shows the current contents of the clipboard.

You'll find some menu commands in Clipboard Viewer that let you work with the clipboard contents:

- *Open* and *Save As* in the File menu let you save the contents in a disk file and retrieve them again later. If you have objects that you use repeatedly (such as a picture for a letterhead or the text of a standard contract clause), you can store them as a gallery clipboard files which you can retrieve quickly and paste where you need them.

- *Delete* in the Edit menu deletes all clipboard contents so the clipboard is empty.

- The list of commands in the Display menu show you all the formats in which the clipboard can place the object it contains. (There may be one or more. The formats are determined by the applications you have installed to run under Windows.) You can choose any one of these formats, so that the client has to accept the object in that format alone, or you can choose *Auto* (which is usually turned on) so that the clipboard offers all possible formats.

Try looking at the clipboard contents now:

1. Switch to Program Manager.

2. Start Clipboard Viewer from the main program group.

   The Clipboard Viewer window opens, showing the square you copied from Paintbrush.

3. Choose *Delete* from the Edit menu and click *Yes* when asked to confirm the deletion.

   The square disappears, and the clipboard is now empty.

4. Double-click Clipboard Viewer's control-menu box to quit Clipboard Viewer.

## Revising Objects

With most Windows programs, once you transfer an object to a client program, you can't easily revise that object. You have to cut the object from the client document, paste it back in a server document where you have the tools to work on the object, revise it, copy it back to the clipboard, and then paste it back into the original client document—an elaborate process at best, confusing at worst.

To make object revision simpler, Windows offers a feature called *embedded objects* in programs that support it. When you paste an object into a program that supports embedded objects, the name of the server program is pasted in with the object itself (thus creating an embedded object). When you double-click the object (or select the object and choose *Edit Object* or a similar command from the Edit menu), Windows automatically starts the server program and puts the object in the program so you can edit it. When you're finished and you quit the program, Windows puts the revised object back into its original place—a much simpler process.

Three programs that come with Windows support embedded objects: Paintbrush, Write, and Cardfile. Because you just pasted an item from Paintbrush into Write, you created an embedded object without knowing it. You can try editing it now to see how it works:

1. Switch to Write and double-click the square box you pasted there.

   The square box momentarily changes color to show that it is selected. Windows starts Paintbrush and loads it with the square box.

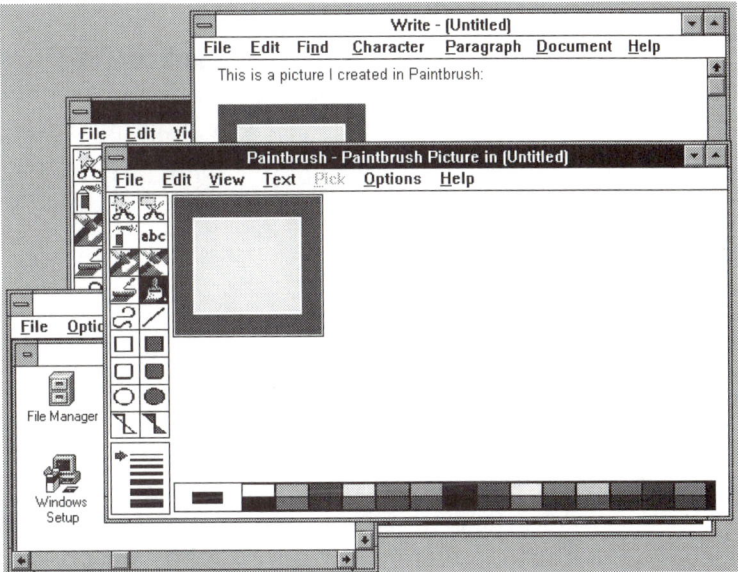

2. Click the filled-rectangle tool in Paintbrush, click the black color in the color strip, then add a third, smaller square in the center of the red square. (If the square is very tiny, the color may not show up.)

3. Quit Paintbrush.

Paintbrush presents a dialog box that asks if you want to update the embedded object before proceeding.

4. Click *Yes*.

Paintbrush quits and the square embedded in your Write document is revised.

Keep in mind that many Windows programs don't support embedded objects, so you'll have to do some tedious transfers back and forth to revise pasted objects. It never hurts to try double-clicking on an object, though. If it is an embedded object, Windows will open the server for you, saving you some tedium.

## Advanced Object Transfers

Simple cutting, copying, and pasting is as advanced as most Windows users need to get when transferring objects between programs. You should know, however, that Windows offers advanced object transfers that are beyond the scope of an introductory book such as this. For example, you can create a picture and save it in a document, paste the picture into a text document, and *link* the embedded picture to its original document. A link sets up the embedded object so that it will always match the contents of the original server document.

Links are useful when you have one object in a server that you paste into many other documents. You can change the original server document, and the pasted copies in all other documents are automatically changed. This seems esoteric, but for users who, for example, put out an annual report with an embedded spreadsheet table, it assures that the report is up-to-date even if somebody goes back and adds new figures to the spreadsheet.

If you're interested in linked objects, you'll find useful information about them in the *Microsoft Windows User's Guide*.

With this look at running several programs at once in Windows, you reach the end of this section on working with programs in Windows. In the next section, you see how to manage your computer system.

# PART III

## MANAGING YOUR COMPUTER SYSTEM

Part III, the last part of this book, shows you how to use Windows to take care of your computer system. You'll see how to move, copy, and delete files that accumulate on your hard disk; how to use some of the advanced features of File Manager; how to manage printing jobs sent to your computer's printer; and how to customize Windows so that it works best for you.

# CHAPTER

# 7

---

# MANAGING FILES, DIRECTORIES, AND DISKS

At some point in your work with Windows, you'll have to do some housecleaning with the files you've stored to disk. It may be the day when you suddenly can't save anything because your hard disk drive is stuffed to the gills and can't hold any more files; it may be the time when you try to find a document in a directory that holds hundreds of confusingly named files; or you may just have an unexpected attack of orderliness. If so, you'll find your cleaning tools in File Manager.

File Manager controls the disks, directories, and files that your computer system uses to store data. You can, as you learned in past chapters, use File Manager to move through the directory trees stored on different disks, looking at the contents of each directory as you move. You can also use File Manager to create your own directories and arrange directory trees to match your own organization; to move or copy files and subdirectories from one directory to another; to rename files and directories; to format and copy floppy disks; and to perform many other file, directory, and disk management tasks.

## Working with Directories

When you run File Manager, it opens with at least one *directory window* (shown in Figure 7-1) visible within its work area. Directory windows are File Manager's document windows; each directory window shows the contents of a single directory and that directory's place in a directory tree. Although many people work with only one directory window open at a time, you can open several at once if you want to compare directory contents (as you'll see later in this chapter).

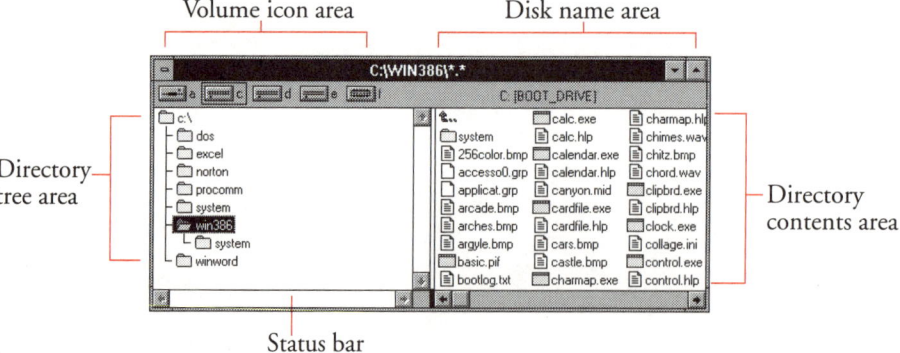

*Figure 7-1*  A directory window displays information about a directory.

The directory window's title bar shows the pathname of the window's current directory; you can also see the current directory outlined in the directory tree. To change to a new directory, simply click on a new directory in the directory tree, and the directory contents area to the right shows the files and subdirectories found in the new directory. If you'd like to change to a directory on another volume, first click on the volume's icon in the volume icon area. When the directory tree for that volume appears, select the directory you want.

## Creating a New Directory

If you'd like to create a new directory, decide where it should go: it has to be a subdirectory of another directory. Select the destination directory in the directory tree (the root directory is fine if you want your directory to stand alone), then choose *Create Directory* from the File menu to open the Create Directory dialog box shown in Figure 7-2. Here you type a directory name in the *Name* text area and then click the OK button. (Note that you must use the same MS-DOS naming rules that you use to name a file, as discussed in Chapter 4.) Your new directory appears—empty of files—in the directory tree.

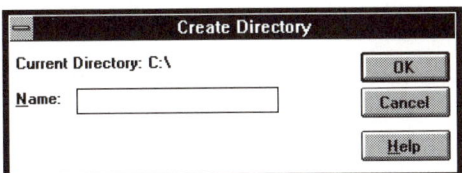

*Figure 7-2* Enter a name for your new directory in the Create Directory dialog box.

Try creating three new directories now as subdirectories of the root directory of your hard disk:

1. Turn on your computer and start Windows, if you haven't done so already.
2. Start File Manager.

   The File Manager window opens and displays at least one directory window.

3. Click on the volume icon for your hard disk drive, if it isn't already selected, then click on the root directory for your drive (located at the top of the directory tree and labeled *c:\* or something similar).

4. Choose *Create Directory* from the File menu.

   The Create Directory dialog box opens.

5. Enter the directory name `letters` in the *Name* text area, then click the OK button to close the dialog box.

   The new directory appears in the directory tree as a subdirectory of the root directory.

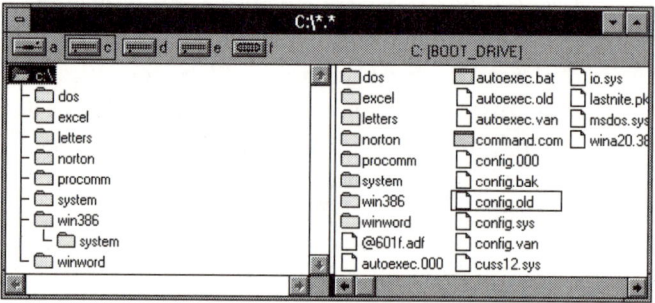

6. Repeat steps 4 and 5, this time entering `personal` to create a directory named *personal.*

   The Personal directory appears as a subdirectory of the root directory.

7. Repeat steps 4 and 5 again, this time entering `business` to create a directory named *business.*

   The Business directory appears as a subdirectory of the root directory.

## Moving a Directory

To move a directory from one location to another, drag the directory from its current location in the directory tree and drop it on the directory where you want to move it. File Manager asks you to confirm the move, you click *Yes,* and the directory becomes a subdirectory of the directory where you dropped it. Try it now with one of the directories you just created:

1. Drag the Personal directory from its position in the directory tree and drop it on the Letters directory.

   File Manager asks you whether you're sure you'd like to move the directory.

2. Click the Yes button.

   The dialog box closes, and the Personal directory becomes a subdirectory of the Letters directory.

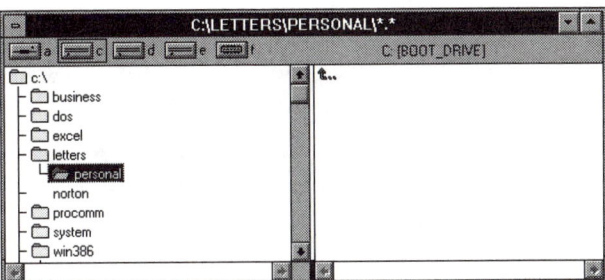

## Copying a Directory

When you copy a directory, you copy all of its files, subdirectories, and files within its subdirectories—quite possibly a massive amount of data, so check the directory's size before you copy, to make sure you won't run out of room on the destination disk drive. From the directory tree, select the directory to copy; File Manager's status bar shows you the number of files in the directory and the total number of bytes used to store them. It does *not* include files stored in subdirectories, so you'll have to click on each subdirectory and add the files there to the total. The left side of the status bar shows how much storage area remains free on the current disk, so you can plan accordingly.

One way to copy a directory is to select the directory in the directory tree and then choose *Copy* from the File menu. File Manager opens a Copy dialog box where you fill in the pathname to the directory where you want to place the copied directory. A simpler way is to hold down the Ctrl key and drag the directory into the destination directory just as you'd copy a file. File Manager asks you to confirm your copy, you click *OK*, and it copies the directory and all of its contents. With either method, it's important to note that you can never copy a directory into a destination directory that is the original directory's parent directory. In other words, you can't copy c:\letters\personal into c:\letters because the Personal directory already exists there.

Try copying the Business directory into the Letters directory:

1. Hold down the Ctrl key, drag *business*, and drop it on *letters*.

   File Manager asks you whether you're sure you want to copy the directory.

2. Click *Yes*.

   The dialog box closes, and a copy of Business becomes a subdirectory of Letters.

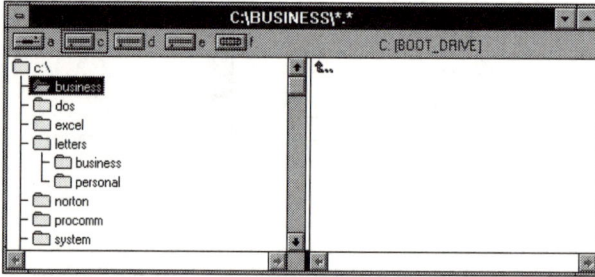

If you want to copy a directory from one disk to another disk, drag the directory and drop it on the volume icon of the disk where you want to copy it. (You don't need to hold down Ctrl while you drag, because File Manager doesn't ever move a file from disk to disk, which would erase the file from its original disk.) For example, if you want to copy a directory from C:, your hard disk, to A:, a floppy disk, find the directory in C:'s directory tree, then drag it and drop it on the icon for A:.

---

**When I Copy to Another Disk, How Do I Know Where the Copied Object Is Stored?**

Whenever you copy a directory or a file by dragging its icon onto a volume icon, the copied object has to take a place within a directory on the destination disk. If the destination disk has many directories, which directory does it go into?

*(continued)*

*Where Is the Copied Object? (continued)*

If you've never looked at the destination disk in File Manager, the copied object goes into the disk's root directory. If you used File Manager to look at the disk and then switched to another disk, File Manager remembers the last selected directory on that disk and puts any objects copied to the disk in that directory. Say, for example, that you selected the directory c:\letters\personal on your hard disk drive and then clicked on *a* to look at the contents of a floppy disk. If you drag a directory or file from the floppy disk and drop it on the c icon to copy it to the hard disk, File Manager places the copied object in the directory c:\letters\personal.

## Renaming a Directory

If you don't like a directory's name, you can easily change it by selecting the directory in the directory tree and choosing *Rename* from the File menu. File Manager opens a dialog box where you can type in the new name and then click on *OK*; the name on the directory is then changed. Try it now to rename your original Business directory to Figures:

1. Click on the original *business* (not the one that's a subdirectory of *letters)* to select it, if it's not already selected.

2. Choose *Rename* from the File menu to open the Rename dialog box.

```
┌─────────────────────────────────────────────────┐
│ ▬                    Rename                       │
├─────────────────────────────────────────────────┤
│ Current Directory: C:\            ┌──────────┐   │
│ From:   [BUSINESS          ]      │    OK    │   │
│                                   └──────────┘   │
│ To:     [                  ]      ┌──────────┐   │
│                                   │  Cancel  │   │
│                                   └──────────┘   │
│                                   ┌──────────┐   │
│                                   │   Help   │   │
│                                   └──────────┘   │
└─────────────────────────────────────────────────┘
```

3. Enter the name figures and press the Enter key (which is the same as clicking *OK*).

The dialog box closes, and Business is now renamed Figures.

## Deleting a Directory

If you want to remove a directory from a disk (perhaps to free up disk space for more files), you select the directory in the directory tree and then choose *Delete* from the File menu to open the Delete dialog box. It shows you the directory you propose to delete. If you click *OK*, it's important to realize that you've asked File Manager to delete *all* the files and subdirectories stored in the directory as well! File Manager fortunately realizes what a big step this is, and asks you to confirm each subdirectory and file before you delete it. It uses the dialog box shown in Figure 7-3.

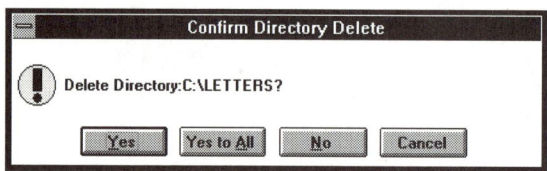

*Figure 7-3* File Manager asks you to confirm each file and subdirectory within a deleted directory before it deletes them.

Note that you have two Yes options: Yes and Yes to All. Click *Yes* if you want to confirm just the file or directory that File Manager proposes to delete. Click *Yes to All* if you want to confirm *every* file or *every* subdirectory within the directory. Yes is a good way to make sure that you don't delete anything important, but it can be tedious, especially if you're deleting a directory containing hundreds of files. Yes to All, on the other hand, can delete a lot of files at once—convenient, but dangerous. Use it with care!

Try deleting the Figures directory now:

1. Click on *figures* in the directory tree to select it, and then choose *Delete* from the File menu.

   The Delete dialog box opens, proposing to delete *C:\FIGURES*.

2. Click *OK* to confirm the deletion.

The Confirm Directory Delete dialog box opens, and asks if it can delete *C:\FIGURES.*

3. Click *Yes.*

Both dialog boxes close and File Manager deletes Figures from the hard disk.

Note that it makes no difference if you select Yes or Yes to All when deleting an empty directory.

# Working with Files

You work with files in File Manager much the same way you work with directories: you click on a file to select it; you choose commands from the File menu to move, copy, rename, or delete a file; you drag files from one directory to another to move or copy a file. If you select a file, you'll find information about its size in File Manager's status bar.

You'll find differences as well. For starters, you can't create an original file in File Manager—you create files in other programs and manage them in File Manager. In addition, you work with files in a different part of a directory window: the directory contents area. Files don't ever appear in the directory tree (although directories appear in the directory contents area). You'll also find that you can perform operations on files that you can't perform on directories: opening, printing, associating, and setting attributes.

## Selecting Files

To select a file in the directory contents area, simply click on the file name. If you want to select a range of files in the area, click on the file name at one end of the range, hold down the Shift key, and then click on the file name at the other end of the range. File Manager selects both files and all the files in between them. Any operations you perform with File commands or by dragging affect all of the selected files.

If you want to select files of a certain type scattered throughout the directory contents area, choose *Select Files* from the File menu to open the Select Files dialog box shown in Figure 7-4. If you enter a file name in the text area and then click *Select*, File Manager selects that file name—a fairly useless operation, considering that you can much more easily click on a file name. This feature's power comes from using *wildcard* characters.

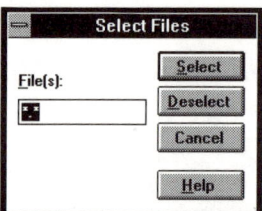

*Figure 7-4* Use the Select Files dialog box to define a group of files you wish to select or deselect.

## What Is a Wildcard Character?

Without getting into full details, a wildcard character is the typed equivalent of someone saying "etcetera" or "whatever"—Windows can fill it in with whatever text it finds. In particular, the character "*" means "any character or group of characters." You can use it before or after the period in a file name to give Windows leeway for that part of the file name.

For example, say you want to specify every file name that ends in .bmp (which is the set of files created by Paintbrush). You enter the file name `*.bmp`, which means "any bunch of characters followed by the extension .bmp". If you enter `avocado.*`, you specify every avocado file, regardless of its extension.

You can use "*" and its wildcard partner "?" (which specifies any *single* character as opposed to any group of characters) to narrowly define a special set of file names—but it takes skill and special knowledge of wildcards, which you can read about in any MS-DOS manual. For most of the work you do in Windows, specifying file types with an asterisk followed by the extension you want (*.bmp, *.exe, and so on) is enough.

By entering a wildcard name in the Select Files dialog box, you can select a group of files that conform to the name you entered. Notice that the dialog box offers both a Select button, which selects files that conform to the file name you set, and a Deselect button, which removes the selection from the files you specify. You can use the Deselect button to deselect specific files from within a range of already selected files. For example, you might select all the files in the directory contents area and then use the Deselect button to deselect all the .exe files, so that every file in the directory except program files is selected.

Try using Select Files to select all the Paintbrush files in the Windows directory:

1. Click on *windows* (or *win386*) in the directory tree to select the directory and see its contents in the directory contents area.

2. Choose *Select Files* from the Files menu to open the Select Files dialog box.

3. Enter the wildcard file name *.bmp to specify all file names ending in .bmp and click *Select*.

   File Manager selects all the Paintbrush files scattered throughout the directory contents area.

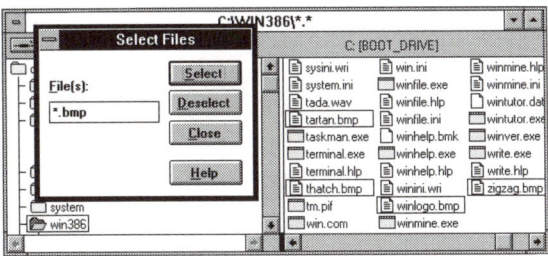

4. Click *Close* to close the dialog box.

## Searching for a File

It's hard to select a file if you can't find it, so File Manager offers a search tool. To use it, choose *Search* from File menu to open the Search dialog box shown in Figure 7-5. If you're searching for a single file, enter the file's name in the Search For text area. If you're searching for a type of file, enter a wildcard file name in the Search

For text area. The dialog box proposes that you search the current directory for your files; you can change the contents of the Start From text area if you want to search through a different directory.

*Figure 7-5* The Search dialog box accepts a regular or wildcard file name and a directory where you want to search for files that match.

The search tool normally searches through the specified directory and goes through each subdirectory (and their subdirectories) to look for files. If you want to restrict the search so that it doesn't go through subdirectories, click on the Search All Subdirectories box to turn it off.

Once you have the search parameters set the way you want them, click *OK* to close the dialog box. File Manager performs the search, and it opens a new directory window to show the results of the search. This directory window contains *only* a directory contents area, which lists every file found in the search and uses the full path-name for each file so you know where it's located. You can close or minimize the window to get it out of the way and return to the directory window you were using before, or—if you want to work directly with the files returned by the search—you can use the File commands in the Search Results window.

## Moving, Copying, and Renaming Files

You move, copy, and rename files using the same techniques you used to move, copy, and rename directories. To move a file, you select it in the directory contents area and then drag and drop it on a destination directory in the directory tree or a destination volume in the volume icon area. To copy a file, you do the same, but hold the Ctrl key down while you're dragging. And to rename a file, you select the file and then choose *Rename* from the File menu so you can enter a new file name.

One handy file variation is that you can move or copy many files at once by dragging a selected group of file names. For example, if you want to copy all the Paintbrush files from the Windows directory onto a floppy disk, you use Select Files to select all files ending in .bmp. You then move your pointer to any one of the selected files and drag it to the location you want—all the other selected files come along with it.

Try copying a file by dragging it:

1. Click on the Windows or Win386 directory to see its contents, if they aren't already visible.

2. Find and click on the file *arches.bmp* to select it.

3. Hold down the Ctrl key and drag *arches.bmp* onto *personal* in the directory tree, drop it, and confirm that you want to copy.

arches.bmp is copied into c:\letters\personal.

## Printing Files

You normally print files from the programs where you create them. For example, if you write a letter in Write, you use the Print command there to print the letter. However, if you don't want to open the creating program to print a file, you can select the file and then choose *Print* from the File menu. File Manager asks you to confirm the file for printing and then opens a Print dialog box where you can set the number of copies and other printing parameters. It then prints the file on your printer. Unfortunately, Windows won't let you print more than one file at a time this way, so you can't select a group of files and ask to print them in one batch.

## Setting File Attributes

Each file you see in File Manager has a set of attributes that controls how the file appears and how you can manipulate it. To set those attributes, first select the file and then choose *Properties* from the File menu to open the Properties dialog box shown in Figure 7-6.

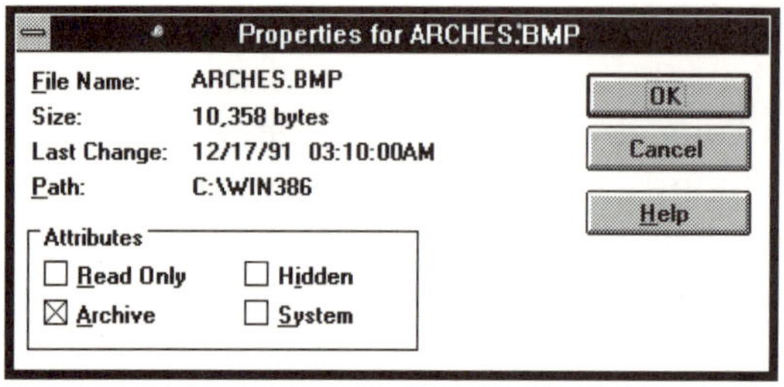

*Figure 7-6* The Properties dialog box shows a file's properties.

You'll find a lot of useful information about the file in the dialog box, including the file size, the time and date it was last changed, and its full pathname. You'll also find four checkboxes where you can turn the file's attributes on and off. They are:

- **Read Only** When turned on, locks the file so you can't change it in another program. If you open a read-only file, edit it, and then try to save it, Windows will inform you that the file is read-only, and won't allow you to save over the original file.

- **Archive** Useful if you use a hard-disk drive backup program (which you should, to protect the contents of your disks from disk failure). If this attribute is turned on, the date and time when the file was last backed up is stored with the file. Most backup programs offer an option to back up only programs that have been modified since the last back up, which needs an archive date to work. If you turn this attribute off, the backup program will automatically back up the file, even if it hasn't been modified since the last backup.

- **Hidden** When turned on, hides the file so it won't appear in the directory contents area of a directory window. You can use this attribute to hide sensitive files or to keep background files from cluttering the file list. You can, as you'll see later, set File Manager to display hidden files without turning this attribute off.

- **System** When turned on, turns the file into a system file (whose file is marked with a red exclamation point). System files don't normally appear in a file list (like hidden files), but you can view them if you wish.

You won't normally change any of these attributes except Read Only, which can protect valuable files from change. If you do change an attribute, you click *OK* to close the dialog box and put the attributes into effect.

# Working with Disks

Although a hard disk drive eliminates the need to work regularly with floppy disks, you'll find that floppy disks are handy for exchanging files with other PC users. You can copy documents to a floppy and then carry or mail it to another PC user, who can insert it and copy the files off the floppy disk. You can also use floppy disks to make backup copies of important files on your hard disk, then store the floppies where they can't come to harm.

File Manager offers a set of disk management tools that help you work with floppy disks as well as hard disks. They can prepare a new floppy disk so you can copy files to it; they can duplicate and label a floppy disk, and, for special purposes, they can create a system disk.

## Formatting a Floppy Disk

When you buy a box of blank new floppy disks, the disks aren't usually prepared for data storage. Before your computer can store data on a floppy disk, the disk must be *formatted*, a process that records a series of magnetic signposts on the disk that help your floppy disk drive find its way to different sectors on the disk. You need to format a floppy disk only once; when the formatting is in place, it stays there even when you erase all the files from that disk.

Formatting a disk is a destructive process—if you format a used disk, formatting wipes out any files that are stored on the disk and leaves you with an empty disk. You can use formatting as a sure-fire way to completely erase files from a disk so they can't be recovered (handy for sensitive data); you can also accidentally use formatting as a way to lose files that you never intended to toss. So be careful and make sure that any disk you format is either new or contains nothing you want to keep. (**Note to DOS 5 users:** You cannot unformat a disk that has been formatted using Windows.)

To format a floppy disk, choose *Format* from the File menu to open the Format Disk dialog box shown in Figure 7-7.

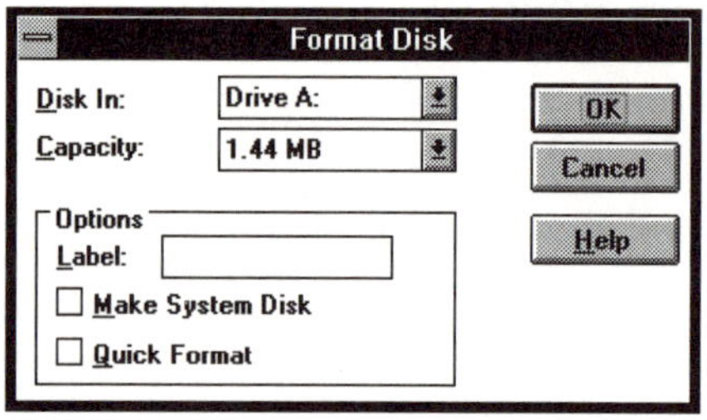

*Figure 7-7* The Format Disk dialog box offers options for formatting a floppy disk.

If you have more than one floppy disk drive in your computer system, you can choose which drive you want to use for formatting by selecting a drive from the Disk In list box at the top of the dialog box. The Capacity list box shows you the capacity options available for your selected drive.

Capacity is determined by your drive's ability to format a disk. Different drives can fit more or less information on the same type of disk. For example, early model 3½-inch floppy disk drives format disks so they can store 720 kilobytes of data; later model drives double that capacity, using a type of formatting that stores 1,440 kilobytes on the same disk. The later drives also offer an option to format disks at 720 kilobytes so that the earlier drives can read disks from later drives.

You normally choose the capacity that gives you the most storage space on a floppy disk. However, if you know that you're sending a disk to somebody whose computer can't read those high-capacity disks, then you should choose a lower capacity to match their drive.

If you want to give your disk a label, you can type it in the Label text area. A label can be up to eleven characters long and can't use spaces or most punctuation marks (much like MS-DOS file name character restrictions). The label is stored on your disk and shows up in the title bar of a directory window when you look at the contents of a disk. Labeling disks can help you quickly remember their contents. For example, you might label a disk *1992_taxes*. (You can use the underline as a convenient replacement for spaces in disk labels and file names.)

The Quick Format option, when turned on, can save you some time when you reformat a used disk. It assumes that your disk has no bad areas on it because it was successfully formatted in the past, so Quick Format doesn't recheck for bad areas while formatting. As a rule of thumb, you shouldn't turn this option on unless you're formatting large numbers of used disks and really need to save time.

The Make System Disk disk option, when turned on, adds to your disk the MS-DOS files needed to start your computer. This makes the disk a system disk. Use this option whenever you need to create a disk for starting a computer. For example, if you're working with a computer that has no hard disk drive, a hard disk drive that doesn't work, or a hard disk drive that—for some reason—won't let you start your computer, you can insert a floppy system disk and start the computer with it. You can then use MS-DOS commands to run programs, look at files on other disks, and operate your computer.

Once you've set the formatting options you want (you usually won't have to set anything because File Manager offers the most standard options already set), you click *OK*, and File Manager asks if you're sure you want to format. When you answer *Yes*, File Manager puts up a small dialog box that shows you the progress of formatting, which usually takes a few minutes. When the format is finished, File Manager asks if you want to format another disk. If so, answer *Yes* and put another disk in the drive. If not, answer *No*, and your formatting is completed.

Try formatting a floppy disk now:

1. Find a new floppy disk or a disk that you don't mind reformatting (check its contents first!) and insert it in a floppy disk drive.

2. Choose *Format Disk* from the Disk menu to open the Format Disk dialog box.

3. If the Disk In list box doesn't display the drive that holds your floppy disk, choose the correct disk drive.

4. Click *OK* to start formatting.

File Manager asks if you're sure you want to proceed.

5. Click *Yes.*

File Manager shows you the results of the formatting as it proceeds. When the disk is formatted, it asks if you want to format another disk.

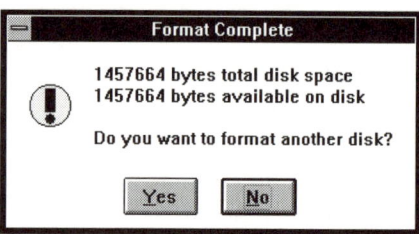

6. Click *No.*

The formatting is finished.

## Automatic Formatting

In a perfect world, all floppy disks would be preformatted straight out of the box, ready for your particular type of disk drive. Unfortunately, there are times when you put a disk in the floppy drive to copy files to it or to look at its contents, and Windows informs you that it's unformatted and can't be read. As a matter of politeness, Windows offers to format the disk for you on the spot.

If you answer *Yes* to the formatting (and you're sure there's nothing on the disk that you don't mind erasing!), you see the standard Format Disk dialog box, where you can set the formatting options you want and then proceed with formatting. When the formatting is finished, Windows continues with the operation you were involved in, completing your file copying or disk query with the now-formatted disk.

## Copying a Floppy Disk

If you'd like to make an exact copy of a floppy disk, File Manager offers a convenient command: Copy Disk in the Disk menu. When you choose it and confirm that you do indeed wish to proceed, File Manager prompts you with the steps you need to take. It first asks you to insert the *source disk,* which is the disk you want to copy. It reads its contents, and then asks you to insert the *destination disk,* which is the blank (or recycled) disk you want to copy to. It copies the contents of the source disk onto the destination disk, and your copy is complete—a simple process.

There is a danger to disk copying that you should avoid: you might accidentally confuse the source and destination disks. If you insert the destination disk first, its blank contents are copied onto your source disk, effectively erasing it. *Be sure to label your disks clearly so you won't confuse them!*

To be even safer, *write-protect* your source disk, which assures that your computer won't format, erase, or write to the disk. To write-protect a $3^1/_2$-inch floppy disk, find the small sliding tab in the corner of the disk and slide it so that the hole behind it is open. To write-protect a $5^1/_4$-inch floppy disk, put a piece of tape over the square notch on the edge of the disk next to the disk label. You can later remove the tape or reset the tab if you want to remove the write protection from the disk.

## Labeling a Disk

If you didn't label a disk during formatting, or want to change its label after it's formatted, insert the disk in a drive, select the disk's volume icon in File Manager, and choose *Label Disk* from the Disk menu to open the Label Disk dialog box shown in Figure 7-8. You can enter a new label in the Label text area and click *OK.* File Manager labels the disk with the text you entered. Note that you can use this command to label hard disks as well as floppy disks.

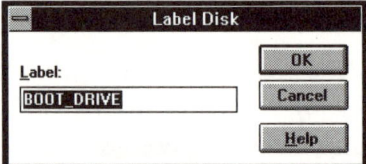

*Figure 7-8* Use the Label Disk dialog box to label or relabel a disk.

# Working with Directory Windows

If you use File Manager infrequently, chances are you'll never need to alter the single directory window presented to you when you first open File Manager. However, if you're a determined file chaser, File Manager offers you some directory window options that can make your work easier.

## Splitting a Directory Window

The standard directory window you use in File Manager is already split into two areas: the directory tree area and the directory contents area. You can change the split to enlarge one area and diminish the other. For example, you can increase the size of the directory contents area (decreasing the size of the directory tree area) to see more file names at one time.

To move the split, move the pointer over the *split bar*, which is the thin vertical border between the two areas in the window. The pointer turns into a thin vertical bar with arrows pointing left and right. Drag the split bar left or right until you've moved the split where you want it, then release the mouse button. Try it now:

1. Move the pointer over the split bar in the directory window.

   The pointer turns into a vertical bar with arrows.

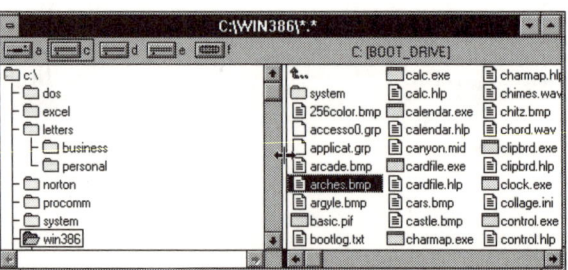

2.  Drag the split bar to the left and release it.

The directory contents area increases, and the directory tree area decreases.

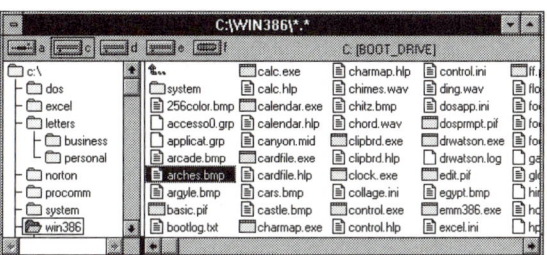

If you'd like to work with a directory window that shows only the directory tree or only directory contents, you can drag the split all the way to the left or right window border, completely eliminating either the directory contents or directory tree area. To split the window again, drag the split from the left or right window border back to the center of the window again. (Note that you can accomplish the same tasks by choosing *Tree Only, Directory Only,* or *Tree and Directory* from the View menu.)

## Directory Tree Options

You learned in Chapter 3 that you can expand and collapse a directory in the directory tree by double-clicking it to see and hide its subdirectories. You'll find some other options in File Manager's Tree menu:

- **Expand Branch**  Opens every subdirectory, subsubdirectory, and so forth within the selected directory, so you can see *every* directory in the branch of the directory tree

- **Expand All**  Shows the complete directory tree for an entire disk, so you can see the full structure of subdirectories stored there

- **Indicate Expandable Branches**  Puts a plus or minus sign on any directory in the directory tree that contains subdirectories. (Directories without subdirectories are blank.) A directory with a plus sign (+) shows that the directory contains hidden subdirectories and can be expanded. A directory with a minus (-) sign shows that the directory is already expanded, displaying its subdirectories in the directory tree.

## File Viewing Options

When you view files in the directory contents area, File Manager usually shows each file as an icon followed by a file name, arranged in alphanumerical order by file name. If the order doesn't suit you, you can change it by choosing another order from the View menu. The order commands are:

- **Sort by Name**  Arranges the files in alphanumerical order
- **Sort by Type**  Arranges the files in order by their type (it sorts their file names alphanumerically by the filename extension)
- **Sort by Size**  Arranges the files in order from the largest file to the smallest file
- **Sort by Date**  Arranges the files in order from the most recently modified file to the file unchanged for the longest period of time.

Choose the order that most suits your needs. For example, if you're trying to find out which files are hogging disk space, sort them by size. Or if you're looking for a file that you know that you worked with last Friday, sort them by date.

If you'd like to see more information for each file than just the icon and file name, try these View commands:

- **Name**  Shows the standard icon and filename for each file
- **All File Details**  Shows name, size, last modification date and time, and all other available information for each file
- **Partial Details**  Opens the Partial Details dialog box shown in Figure 7-9. You can turn on only the file details you'd like to see and click *OK*; File Manager shows those details for each file.

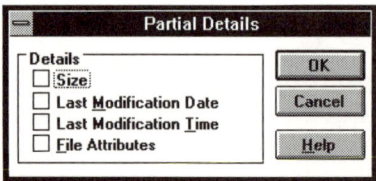

*Figure 7-9*  In the Partial Details dialog box, turn on the options that you'd like displayed for each file.

If you're interested in only a certain type of file, you can filter the files that File Manager displays so you won't have to look through other file types. To filter, choose *By File Type* from the View menu to open the By File Type dialog box shown in Figure 7-10.

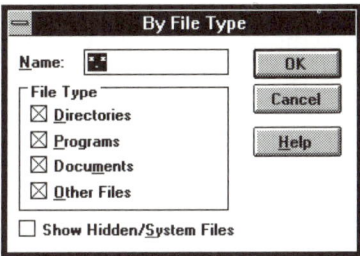

*Figure 7-10* The options in the By File Type dialog box determine which files appear in the directory contents area and which files don't.

To filter by file name, enter a wildcard file name in the *Name* text area. For example, the wildcard file name *\*.bmp* will display only files whose names end in .bmp, so that you see only bitmap picture files. To filter by file type, turn on the types you'd like to see in the File Type area. They are:

- **Directories**  Shows directories
- **Programs**  Shows files that you can run as a program (typically files whose names end in .exe, .com, or .bat)
- **Documents**  Shows files, such as letters or pictures that were created by programs such as Write or Paintbrush
- **Other Files**  Shows any files that aren't programs, documents, or directories.

And if you'd like to see hidden files and system files that aren't usually displayed, turn on the Show Hidden/System Files option.

Once you've set the characteristics of the files you'd like to see in the directory window, click *OK,* and File Manager then shows only those types of files in the directory contents area, even when you switch from directory to directory. To turn the filtering off, set the By File Type dialog box so the *Name* is *\*.\*,* turn on every File Type option, turn off the Show Hidden/System Files option, and click *OK.*

## Working with Multiple Directory Windows

File Manager can open more than one directory window at a time within its main window, so you can look at the contents of two or more directories at once if you wish. You can drag icons back and forth among open directory windows, so multiple directory windows make it easy to copy items from one disk to any directory on a second disk. For example, if you open one directory window showing files on disk A: (your floppy disk drive) and a second showing the directory tree on disk C: (your hard disk drive), you can drag a file from A: to C: and copy it to precisely the directory you want.

To open a new directory window, you can either choose *New Window* from the Window menu, which duplicates the active document window, or you can double-click on any volume icon, which opens a document window showing the contents of that volume.

Once you have two or more document windows open, you handle them just as you do document windows in other Windows applications: click on a window to make it active; minimize a window to an icon to get it out of the way; choose *Cascade* or *Tile* from the Window menu to arrange open windows; and choose *Arrange Icons* from the Window menu to arrange icons along the bottom of the File Manager window.

Try opening a second document window now so you can copy a file from one window to another:

1. Click on the a volume icon to show the contents of the floppy disk you just formatted.

2. Double-click on the c volume icon.

   File Manager opens a second directory window showing the contents of disk C:.

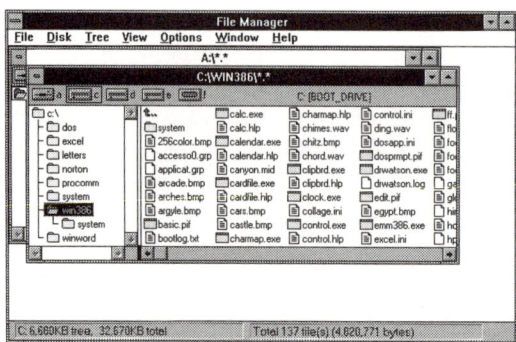

3. If necessary, click on the double arrow in the C: directory window to make the display smaller.

4. Click on *windows* (or *win386*) in the C: directory tree to see the contents of that directory.

5. Drag the C: window to the left to reveal the directory tree in the A: window.

6. Hold down the Ctrl key and drag *arches.bmp* from the directory contents area of the second window onto the *a:\* directory in the directory tree of the first window and drop the file there.

   When you press Enter at the Confirm Mouse Operation dialog box, File Manager copies the file from disk C: to the root directory of the floppy disk in drive A:.

7. Close the A: drive window and eject the floppy disk from the floppy disk drive.

# Customizing File Manager

When you work with Program Manager, you can customize it so that it presents the best possible working environment for starting programs. You can do the same with File Manager. In fact, you'll find many more customization options in File Manager than you did in Program Manager.

## Setting the Confirmation Level

You may have noticed that File Manager takes time to make sure that you really want to go ahead with the actions you propose. This is a sort of safety net to make sure that you don't accidentally erase an entire directory when you want to erase a single file or otherwise irrevocably change files on your disks. If you'd like to speed up File Manager's operations, you can turn off confirmation—but be prepared to live with the risk.

To change confirmation, choose *Confirmation* from the Options menu to open the Confirmation dialog box shown in Figure 7-11. All the confirmations are normally turned on; you can click on any of them to turn them off.

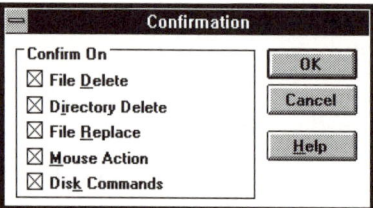

*Figure 7-11* Turn off options in the Confirmation dialog box to bypass confirmation notices and speed up operations in File Manager.

The first three types of confirmations control whether File Manager confirms file deletions, directory deletions, or file replacements. Mouse Action confirms any drag and drop actions you take with the mouse (such as moving or copying files or directories), and Disk Commands confirms disk formats and disk copies.

Once you've set the confirmations as you want them, click *OK* to close the dialog box and put them into effect.

## Setting the Font

File Manager usually displays file and directory names in lowercase text using small characters. If you have trouble reading them or you find them ugly, you can set a new *font* (the character and size of letters) that is easier to look at. Choose *Font* from the Options menu to open the Font dialog box shown in Figure 7-12.

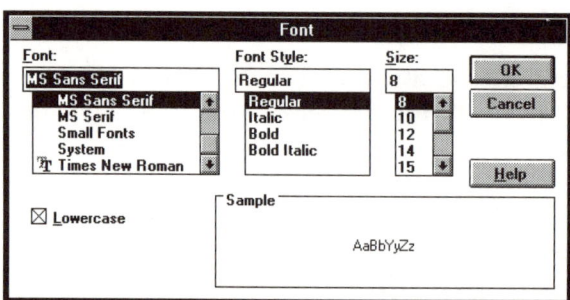

*Figure 7-12* The options in the Font dialog box control the appearance of text in the File Manager window.

You can choose elements in three combo boxes: Font, Font Style, and Size. The names in the Font box control the character of the letters—from smooth and curved to blocky and stark. The Font Style names control the weight of the characters: Regular, Bold or Italic for emphasis, or combined Bold Italic for even more emphasis. And the Size choices control the point size of the characters: the higher the number, the larger the characters.

As you choose different settings in these three boxes, the Sample area in the lower right of the dialog box shows how the text will look with those settings. You can experiment until you get just the text you want.

Before you put a new font into effect by clicking *OK*, you have one more option you can control: the Lowercase check box, which controls upper- and lowercase display in File Manager. When it's turned on, all directory and file names appear in lowercase, something like an e. e. cummings poem. When it's turned off, all names appear in uppercase, imposing but perhaps easier to read.

## Turning the Status Bar on and off

The status bar at the bottom of the File Manager window gives you information about selected directories and files. If you want to get rid of it so the window has more workspace, choose *Status Bar* from the Options menu. Choose it again to turn it on.

## Saving Your File Manager Setup

If you've set up a directory window arrangement with directories open where you want them and directory trees arranged to taste, you can make sure that your arrangement is saved when you exit File Manager—make sure *Save Settings on Exit* is turned on in the Options menu. Once you've quit File Manager to save your arrangement and then started File Manager again, turn *Save Settings on Exit* off so you'll start with the same arrangement. This feature works exactly like the equivalent command in Program Manager.

You've now seen how to handle File Manager's most powerful tools; you should be able to use File Manager to keep your disks and files in order, and to share files with other computer users via floppy disks.

Before you quit, take a minute to clean up the directories and files you created for the examples in this chapter:

1.  Select *letters* in the directory tree of the C: drive.

2.  Choose *Delete* from the File menu to delete the directory and all of its contents.

    File Manager shows you *C:\LETTERS* as the directory to delete.

3.  Click *OK.*

    File Manager asks you to confirm your deletion.

4.  Click *Yes to All* to delete directories and again to delete files.

    File Manager deletes Letters and all the files and directories it includes.

You're now free and clear to proceed to the next chapter on printing.

# CHAPTER
# 8

---

# MANAGING PRINTING

When all works smoothly in Windows, printing is a simple matter: You open a document in an application, choose *Print* from the File menu, and forget about it until the document slides out of your printer on sheets of paper. As long as your printing needs aren't extensive, there's no reason why printing can't be this simple. If, however, you print many documents at a time, use more than one printer, or your printer runs out of paper in the middle of a printing job, printing demands a bit more of your attention.

This chapter shows you the techniques you need to handle extensive printing. You'll see how to use Print Manager, a Windows application dedicated to printing, and you'll find ways to fine-tune printing so that your printer and your computer can both run at optimal speed.

## Understanding Print Manager

Whenever you print a document from an application, the application sends a stream of data to your printer—characters, lines, textures, and other information necessary to make your printer lay down on paper the document that you see on your monitor. The printer digests the data and begins printing, a process that's usually quite slow compared to your computer's speed, because it's limited by the mechanics of printing or—in some cases—extensive calculations to create complex pictures or figures.

An application running under MS-DOS alone is severely limited by slow printing speed. Because MS-DOS doesn't support multitasking, the application is tied up feeding data to the printer for as long as it takes a document to print. You can't do more work with the application until the document is finished.

An application running under Windows has, fortunately, an easier time of it. When it prints, it quickly sends the printing data stream to Print Manager, a Windows application dedicated to printing. Print Manager stores the printing data on disk as a *print job*. The application is then off the printing hook and goes back to other work, such as sorting records or accepting input from you. Print Manager, in the meantime, runs in the background (thanks to Windows' multitasking ability), spooling the contents of the print job from the disk to the printer as fast as the printer can take it.

If you print another document while Print Manager is already at work on a print job, Print Manager pauses printing, stores the incoming print data on disk as a second print job, and then continues printing the first print job. Print Manager can accept and store many print jobs—it lines them up for printing in a waiting list called a *print queue.* Print Manager works through the print jobs in the order in which it received them and, when finished, quits until another application requests Print Manager to print a document.

You can, at any time while Print Manager is running, open the Print Manager window (shown in Figure 8-1) and look at the current print queue. While there, you can choose commands that allow you to pause and resume printing, change the order of the print jobs in the queue, or even remove a print job from the queue entirely.

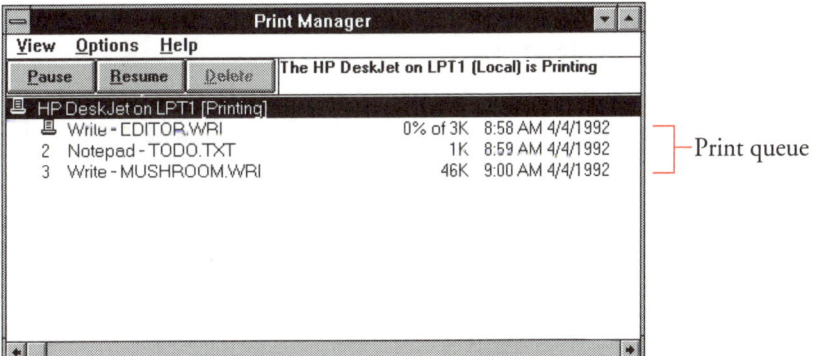

*Figure 8-1* The Print Manager window shows the order of print jobs in the print queue and lets you control the printing process.

You can also use Print Manager to set *default printer options*—that is, printer settings such as paper size and print quality that are used for every print job unless you specifically ask for different settings. If you have more than one printer attached to your computer, one of the most important options you can set here is the *default printer*— the printer to which all print jobs normally go.

If your computer is connected to a computer network, it may have access to many different printers spread throughout the net. If so, Print Manager ties you into those printers and lets you look at the print queue for each printer, which consists of print jobs sent to it from other printer users connected to the net. Network printing is an advanced topic that an introductory book such as this can't cover. If you're interested in the details, your system administrator can help you, or you can find them in the manuals that come with Windows.

## Starting Print Manager

You can start Print Manager in one of two ways: automatically, by printing a document from an application; or manually, by double-clicking its icon in the Main group of Program Manager. When you start Print Manager automatically by printing, Print Manager appears as an icon at the bottom of the desktop, where it remains until it's finished printing. It then quits and disappears.

If you want to use Print Manager once it's started automatically, simply double-click its icon to open the Print Manager window. You can then look at the print queue and issue any printing commands you care to give.

Try starting Print Manager now and putting three print jobs in its queue. For this example, keep your printer turned off so that printing is stalled and Print Manager remains running.

1. Turn on your computer and start Windows, if you haven't already done so.

2. Use Program Manager to start Write.

3. Type some text, such as, `This is a simple document for printing.`

4. Choose *Print* from the File menu.

   The Print dialog box opens. (Note that the Print dialog box varies depending on the kind of printer you have attached to your computer. The one shown below is the Print dialog box for a Hewlett-Packard DeskJet printer.)

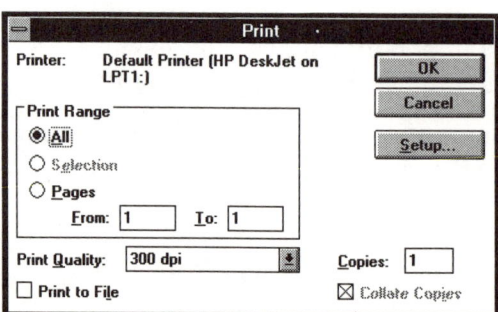

5. With your printer turned *off,* click *OK* to start printing.

   The Print dialog box closes, and a small dialog box briefly opens to inform you that the application is printing. Print Manager starts, its icon appears at the bottom of the desktop, and a dialog box appears to tell you that your printer is either disconnected or out of paper (which isn't quite true— it's just turned off).

6. Ignore the warning: Click *Cancel* to close the dialog box.

7. Start Notepad from Program Manager and type something simple in it for printing.

8. Choose *Print* from Notepad's File menu.

   A dialog box informs you that your printer is disconnected or out of paper.

9. Click *Cancel* to close the dialog box.

10. Switch back to Write and print the document there once again, clicking *Cancel* to close the printer disconnect notice when it appears.

You've now started Print Manager and given it three print jobs, two from Write and one from Notepad. Because the printer is off, printing is stalled, the jobs remain frozen in the print queue, and Print Manager remains in operation.

---

### Setting Special Printing Options for a Single Document

Print Manager normally prints your documents using its default printing options—probably set to use standard paper and the best printing quality. What do you do if you want to print a document using different options? You choose *Print Setup* from the File menu of the application (or from the options menu of Print Manager) to open the Print Setup dialog box, a sample of which is shown in Figure 8-2.

*(continued)*

*Setting Special Printing Options for a Single Document (continued)*

The Print Setup dialog box varies from printer to printer, offering options that match the capabilities of your particular printer. The options are set to the default options as they've been defined in Print Manager. If you want different settings, change them and click *OK* to put them into effect. When you print the document, Print Manager uses your special settings for the document.

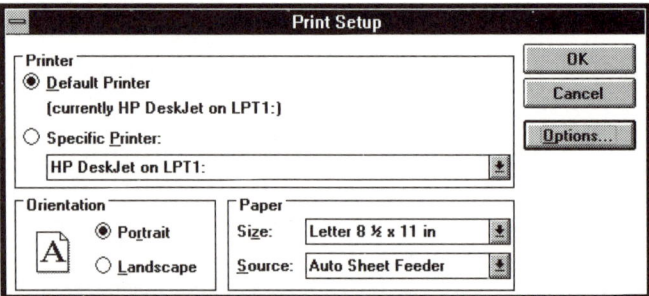

*Figure 8-2*  Use the Print Setup dialog box to set special printing options for a document.

Your special settings remain in effect for the application until you quit, so change them back if you want to print further documents using default settings. If you quit the application and start it again later, it automatically returns to default printing settings.

## Managing the Print Queue

Once Print Manager is started, you can open its window to check the print queue, as shown in Figure 8-3. At the top of the print queue, you'll find the printer listing, which tells you the name of the printer, the port where the printer is connected, and the printer's current status. Chances are that the port will be LPT1, the standard printer plug on the back of your computer. The status may read *Idle*, which means the printer has no work to do; *Printing*, which means the printer is at work; or *Stalled*, which means the printer is out of paper, disconnected, turned off, or otherwise unable to work on print jobs.

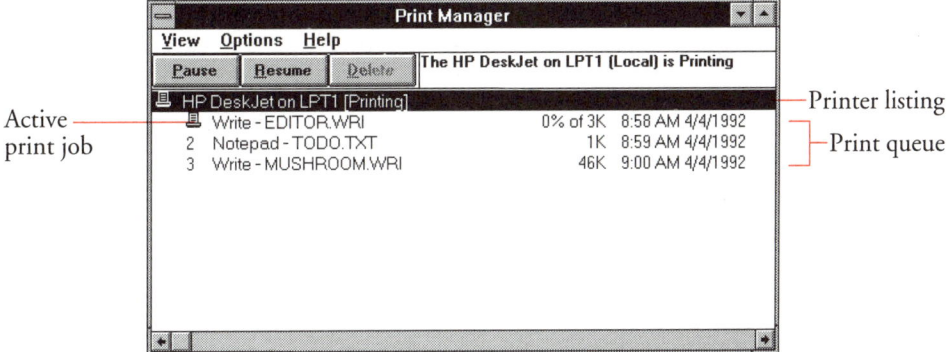

*Figure 8-3* The Print Manager window shows the print queue topped by the printer listing of the printer working on the queue.

The print jobs in the print queue are lined up beneath the printer listing and numbered in the order in which they'll be printed. The top job—marked with a small printer icon—is the active job, the job now being spooled to the printer. The jobs listed below are waiting their turn for printing. Whenever Print Manager finishes a print job, it removes the job from the top of the queue and starts on the next job.

To help you identify different print jobs, each job listing in the print queue includes the name of the application that sent the print job, the name of the document (if it's named), the size of the print job file, and the time and date when the print job was sent to Print Manager. Note that you can choose *Time/Date Sent* or *Print File Size* from the View menu to turn off (and on) the information about file size and time, but there's no real reason to do so.

## Pausing and Resuming Printing

If you need to stop printing before a document is finished (perhaps to freeze the print queue briefly or to interrupt a very large print job), select the printer listing in the print queue, then click the Pause button above the print queue. Print Manager puts a hand icon before the printer listing to show that the printer is paused, and it stops spooling data to the printer. (Your printer may continue printing for a while afterwards, however, because it has data left in its own memory. It will stop as soon as it runs out of data.) To resume printing, click the Resume button next to the Pause button.

## Changing the Order of Print Jobs in the Queue

Although Print Manager handles print jobs in the order in which they're received, you can change the order of all the jobs in the print queue—with the exception of the active job, listed at the top of the queue. It must remain in place because it's in the middle of being printed. It can't be removed without deleting it.

To change the order of a print job waiting in the queue, simply drag it to a new queue location. When you move the pointer on top of the print job, you'll see it turn into an upward pointing arrow, which means that you can drag the print job. As you drag, an outline of the job moves up or down the print queue. Drop it when you get it to the position you want, and the print job moves to that location. Dragging a print job up the print queue is a very handy way to get an important document printed without waiting for every other document in the queue to print first.

## Deleting a Print Job

At some time or other, you'll want to delete a print job from the print queue. You may realize that you left out an important fact in a letter, or that you accidentally set printing to give you 22 copies of a document when you only wanted two. If so, click on the job to select it, then click the Delete button above the queue. Print Manager will ask you to confirm the deletion, and then remove the job from the queue if you confirm. Once the job is deleted, you can't retrieve it, so be sure that you want to delete it. Note that you can delete the active job if you wish, which stops its printing and moves Print Manager on to the next job in the queue.

Now try working with the print queue. Change the order of jobs in the print queue, delete the active print job, and then pause and resume printing:

1. Double-click the Print Manager icon to open its window.

2. Drag print job 3 (labeled *3 Write - (Untitled)*) up until its outline appears in the second queue position.

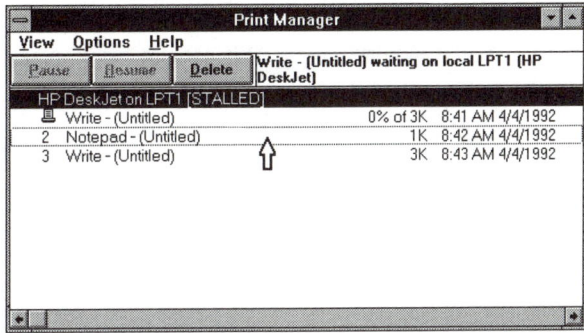

3. Drop the print job.

   The print job moves up the queue from the third position to the second position.

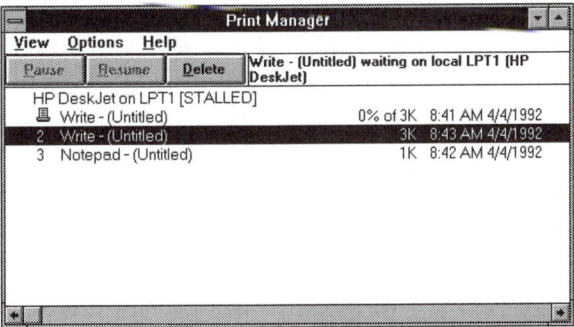

4. Select the active print job at the top of the print queue (labeled with a small printer icon to its left), then click *Delete*.

   A dialog box appears asking if you want to stop printing the print job.

5. Click *OK*.

   The dialog box closes, and Print Manager deletes the print job from the queue. The next print job moves up to take its place as the active print job, and Print Manager informs you once again that the printer is disconnected or out of paper.

6. Click *Cancel* to close the message dialog box.

7. Select the printer listing just above the active print job.

8. Click *Pause* to pause printing.

An upheld hand icon appears to the left of the printer listing, and the listing normally says the printer is paused. The Print Manager no longer tries to spool text to the printer.

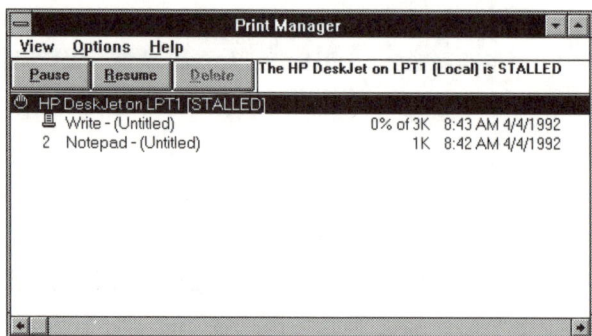

9. Turn your printer on and make sure that it's selected. (Most printers are automatically selected when turned on and show it with a lit "Selected," "Online," or "Ready" light. If your printer isn't selected, you may have to press a Select button or read your printer manual to find out how to select it.)

10. Click the Resume button.

The hand disappears from the printer listing, which now shows printer status as *Printing*. Your printer prints the two documents, emptying the print queue. When finished, the printer listing shows printer status as *Idle*.

## Handling Print Messages

If you print while your printer is turned on, selected, and full of paper, then Print Manager should handle your print job and quit without fanfare when finished. However, circumstances may unexpectedly stop the Print Manager, in which case it will ask you to take some action. You saw how this worked when you tried printing with your printer turned off; Print Manager presented a dialog box that said your printer was disconnected or out of paper and suggested that you fix it. If you had fixed it (by turning it on, in this case), you could then click the Resume button, and Print Manager would continue printing.

Print messages such as this are usually sent by Print Manager for one of two reasons: the printer is no longer accepting data (in which case Print Manager assumes the printer is disconnected or out of paper); or the printer sends a message back to Print Manager that demands attention. Print Manager handles the two types of situations in different ways.

When the printer is no longer accepting data, Print Manager pops up a dialog box that informs you, so you can fix the situation. This dialog box appears as soon as the data flow is jammed—Print Manager thinks it's important, so it interrupts whatever you're working on to let you know.

When the printer sends a message back to your computer, Print Manager's response isn't always as urgent. Because these messages usually don't signal a printing catastrophe (they may ask you to insert a new envelope or sheet of paper, if you're hand-feeding your printer, or they may inform you that the printer's memory is low), Print Manager's usual way to deal with the message is to flash the Print Manager icon off and on, or, if the Print Manager window is open, to flash the window's title bar. This is a gentle request for you to go to the Print Manager window, read the print message there, and take appropriate action.

If this gentle persuasion is too much or not enough for your taste, you can change the way Print Manager presents print messages by choosing one of three commands from the Options menu:

- **Alert Always** Sets print messages to appear in a dialog box as soon as they occur, even if Print Manager isn't the active program. In other words, they appear even if you're working in another application.

- **Flash if Inactive** The normal setting, which sets the Print Manager icon or window title bar to flash if a print message occurs while Print Manager isn't the active program.

- **Ignore if Inactive** Sets print messages to wait inside Print Manager until you come to Print Manager as the active program. If a print message occurs while you're working in another program, you won't see any flashing to let you know there's a message waiting. You have to go back to Print Manager to check from time to time for messages.

# Controlling Printing Speed

Windows' ability to multitask makes Print Manager as useful as it is —it can print in the background while you work with another application. However, as you learned in Chapter 6, multitasking has a potential drawback: When one program gets busy, other programs running at the same time tend to slow down along with the busy program. You'll often notice this while printing. If Print Manager sends a particularly involved document to a printer (for example, it sends digitized pictures to a laser printer), it can significantly slow down all other Windows applications, making your typing in a word processor an excruciating exercise in patience.

To fine-tune the way Print Manager works with other multitasking programs, you can set Print Manager's priority to speed up printing at the expense of other programs or to slow down printing so that other programs will run faster. Three commands in the Options menu control printing priority:

- **Low Priority**  Asks Print Manager to take a back seat to other applications. This slows down printing but makes your work in other applications go more quickly.

- **Medium Priority**  The normal setting, which gives Print Manager equal footing with other programs, so printing and other application tasks are balanced—printing slows down other programs, and other programs slow down printing.

- **High Priority**  Gives Print Manager permission to print at the expense of applications. This speeds up printing and slows down your work in other applications.

Choose the priority that works best for you. If you really need to get printing done quickly, High Priority is a good choice, even though it may slow down your other work. If printing isn't urgent, Low Priority will slow it down, so your own work will go faster. Note that if you aren't doing any other work besides printing on the computer, printing priority isn't important; no matter what the setting, all the computer's time is devoted to printing.

# Setting Default Printer Settings

Whenever you print a document through Print Manager, it prints using default printer settings, unless you specify special settings using the Print Setup command in the application where you printed the document. If you don't like the current printer default settings—perhaps you always print on legal size paper, but the default specifies standard paper, for example—you can change default settings from the Printers dialog box shown in Figure 8-4.

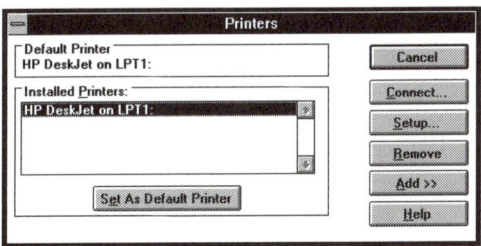

*Figure 8-4* The Printers dialog box shows connected printers and lets you change their default settings.

To open the Printers dialog box, choose *Printer Setup* from the Options menu of Print Manager. Once there, select a printer (if there's more than one) from the Installed Printers list, then click *Setup* to open an options dialog box for that printer. Figure 8-5 shows a typical example.

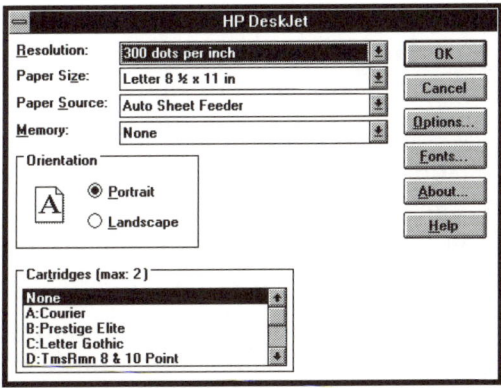

*Figure 8-5* The Printer Setup command opens an options dialog box with options for your printer. This dialog box shows options available for a Hewlett-Packard DeskJet printer. Your printer may have a completely different dialog box.

The default options you may set depend entirely on the capabilities of your printer. Typical options include the size of paper with which you print, the resolution (quality) of printing, and the orientation of printing on the paper (vertical or horizontal, labeled *Portrait* and *Landscape*). You'll have to read your printer manual to understand how each of the options works.

Once you change options to the settings you'll use most often (remember that you can override some of them for individual documents), click *OK* to close the dialog box, then click *OK* again to close the Printers dialog box. All documents you print afterward will use those settings, unless you specifically ask otherwise.

# Working with More Than One Printer

You may be one of the rare computer users who is fortunate enough to have more than one printer attached to your computer—perhaps because you have an expensive printer for color graphics and fine printing and an inexpensive printer for all other work, or perhaps just because you turn out reams of paperwork and need all the help you can get. Whatever the reason, you can easily use Print Manager to handle print jobs for any and all printers connected to your computer.

## Setting a Default Printer

To see what connected printers Windows knows about, choose *Printer Setup* from the Print Manager Options menu to open the Printers dialog box and look in the Installed Printers list box.

If an attached printer isn't listed here, it hasn't been *installed*—that is, the printer driver necessary to run it hasn't been copied onto your hard disk, and Windows hasn't been made aware of the printer's presence. You can install a new printer using the Add button (see Appendix A, *Installing Windows*).

Windows uses one printer from all installed printers as the default printer—the printer to which all print jobs normally go. The default printer is listed in the Default Printer area. To change the default printer, select the printer you'd like in the Installed Printers list box, then click the Set As Default Printer button. The new printer appears in the Default Printer area.

## Specifying a Non-Default Printer for a Document

When you print a document from an application, you can specify a different printer than the default printer, a useful option if the default printer is busy or it doesn't have the features you want for printing the document. To do so, choose *Print Setup* from the application's File menu to open the Print Setup dialog box shown in Figure 8-6.

In the Printer area at the top of the dialog box, you'll find the Specific Printer option followed by a list box that, when open, shows all installed printers. Open the list box, then click on the printer you want. The list box closes, and the Specific Printer option is set. Click *OK* to close the dialog box. Any documents you print in the application then go to printer you just chose.

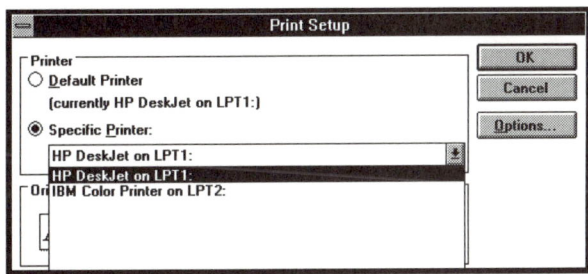

*Figure 8-6* The Print Setup dialog box offers you a choice of printers, if you have more than one printer installed on your computer.

## Viewing Multiple Print Queues

If you send documents to different printers and then open the Print Manager window, you'll see multiple print queues—one for each printer—as shown in Figure 8-7. At the top of each print queue is a printer listing to identify the print queue. All print jobs listed beneath the printer listing are waiting to be printed on that printer.

If you'd like to pause printing on a particular printer, select its printer listing and then click *Pause* or *Resume*. Print Manager stops printing only for the selected printer and continues printing to the other printers. If you'd like to change the order of print jobs in a queue, drag them to new positions—but be aware that you can't drag a job from one printer's queue into another printer's queue. This feature protects each printer from trying to interpret printing data created for a completely different type of printer.

To delete print jobs, use the same technique that you do with a single print queue: select a job and then click *Delete*.

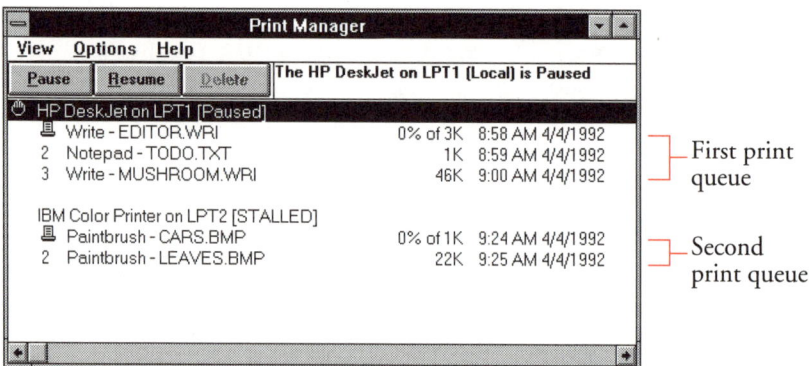

*Figure 8-7* Print Manager presents multiple print queues when it has print jobs waiting for more than one printer.

Now that you've peered into Print Manager's window and seen how it handles print jobs, you should be equipped to handle the minor emergencies that crop up from time to time while printing. You can also tweak Print Manager to print documents the way you like them and to set printing speed to your satisfaction. In the next chapter, you'll see how to tune up Windows itself to create your own personal working environment.

# CHAPTER

# 9

---

# CUSTOMIZING
# WINDOWS

It's only human to try to make your workplace more comfortable, a place that fits your style of work. In a room, you can hang posters, bring in a light that you like, and put your phone close at hand. On a computer system, you're traditionally limited to whatever dull corporate tones the operating system publisher chooses to give you. So it's a pleasant surprise that the normally staid folks at Microsoft decided to let loose a little bit with Windows and give you the tools to customize it.

This chapter is a brief introduction to those tools. It doesn't go into great detail (there are too many customization options for a introductory text like this one), but it does introduce you to the most common and useful types of customization. At the very least, you'll see how to turn Windows into a set of wildly flamboyant colors. With a little experimentation, you'll fine-tune Windows until it looks and works just the way you like it.

## Control Panel

The tools you use to customize Windows are all found in Control Panel (shown in Figure 9-1). You start Control Panel from the Main program group in Program Manager and use it to start different *options,* each of which controls a different type of customization.

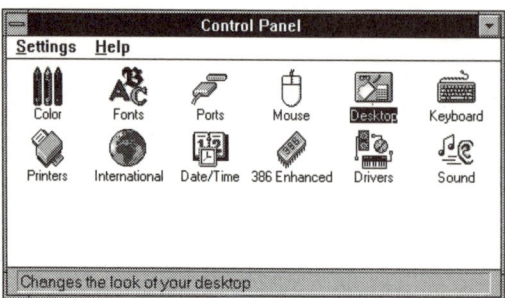

*Figure 9-1* Control Panel provides a variety of options to customize Windows.

Each option is represented within the Control Panel window by an icon. The options you see can vary from computer to computer because Windows, when installed, puts up only the options that apply to your system. For example, only computers connected to a network include the Network option. Only computers with a MIDI controller include the MIDI Mapper option. The options that you read about here, however, are common to almost every computer.

To use an option, double-click the option's icon in Control Panel or (if you're mouseless) choose the option's name from the Settings menu. An option window opens with customization controls that you can set. Once you're finished, click *OK* to close the option window, and your settings go into effect.

# Setting Windows Colors

One of the flashiest changes you can make to Windows is to specify a new collection of colors for window borders, title bars, text, and other elements you see laid out on the desktop—including the desktop itself. You'll find the colors available in the Color option window shown in Figure 9-2, which you open by double-clicking the Color icon.

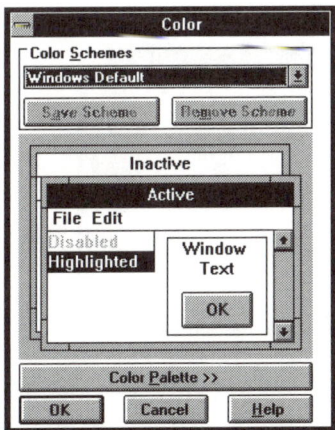

*Figure 9-2* Use the settings in the Color window to change Windows' colors.

At the top of the window, in the list box labeled *Color Schemes*, you can browse through a collection of preset color sets called *color schemes*. Each color scheme is a coordinated set of colors for Windows elements. To see a color scheme, click a scheme name in the list; its colors appear in the sample element layout just below the Color Schemes area. The layout includes all the standard Windows elements—desktop, window borders, title bars, window text, and so on—so you can see how the colors work together.

As you browse through color schemes, you can find gaudy schemes like Fluorescent and Hotdog Stand, subdued schemes like Tweed and Wingtips, and many other schemes to fit your taste. Several of these schemes are designed specifically to make Windows look good on a monochrome monitor or on the display of a laptop computer. The Monochrome color scheme looks good on a monochrome monitor; Plasma Power Saver is designed for a plasma display adapter; and the three schemes starting with *LCD* work well on the LCD (Liquid Crystal Display) screens used primarily on laptop computers. You can sample them to see which works best on your display.

Try setting a new color scheme now:

1. Turn on your computer and start Windows, if you haven't done so already.

2. Start Control Panel from the Main program group of the Program Manager.

   The Control Panel window opens.

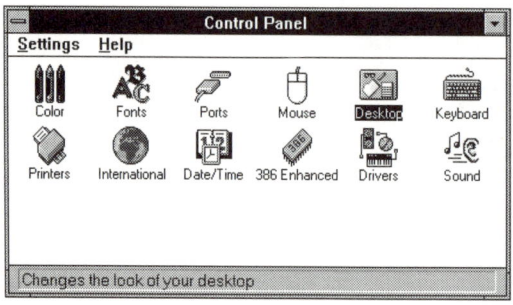

3. Double-click the Color icon to open the Color window.

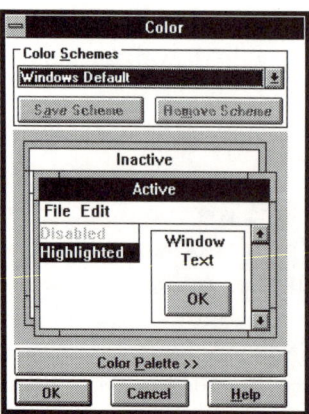

4. Click the Color Schemes list box arrow to open the list box.

5. Find and click on the color scheme titled *Hotdog Stand*.

   The sample element layout below changes to show elements in red, yellow, white, and black (at least it does if you have a color monitor).

6. Click *OK* to close the Colors window and apply Hotdog Stand to Windows.

   Your windows and desktop now appear in hot, gaudy colors.

If you can't stand Hotdog Stand (which is understandable), go back and choose another color scheme that you do like. If you want to return to the original color scheme, choose *Windows Default*, which is the color scheme that Windows uses when first installed.

## Creating a Custom Color Scheme

You might not like any of the color schemes that come with Windows. If so, you can make your own scheme, mixing and matching colors provided by Windows, or creating colors of your own. To do so, open the Color window, then click the Color Palette button in the lower part of the window to expand the window and see available colors, as shown in Figure 9-3.

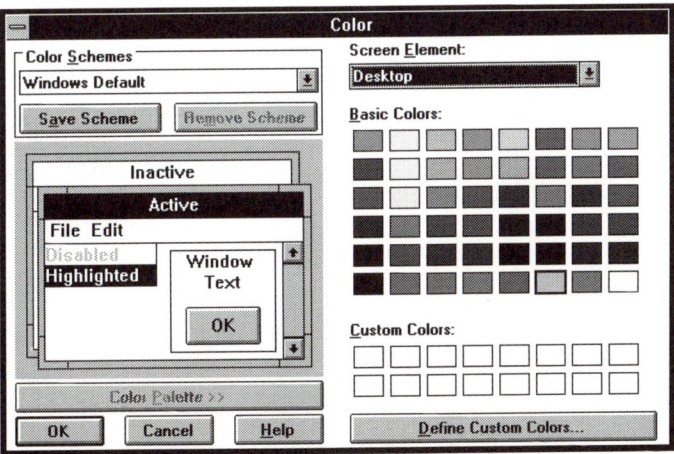

*Figure 9-3* The expanded Color window offers a palette of colors that you can use to create your own color scheme.

You might best start by choosing a Windows color scheme that's close to what you want. You can then alter it. To change the color of a Windows element, first select the element (by clicking it in the sample element's display or by choosing its name from the Screen Element list box) and then select a color from the Basic Colors palette. The element then displays your selected color.

If you don't find the colors you want in the Basic Colors palette, you can make your own colors by clicking on a Custom Color box at the bottom of the screen (which all start out empty of color), then clicking the Define Custom Colors button. This opens the Custom Color Selector window (shown in Figure 9-4), which offers a rectangle filled with a color spectrum.

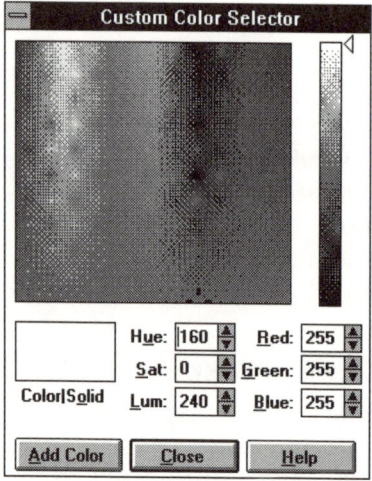

*Figure 9-4* You can create your own colors in the Custom Color Selector window.

You can very simply create a color by clicking in the rectangle where you see the color you want and then clicking *Add Color* to put the color in the selected custom color box. Click *Close* to leave the color selection window. (If you want finer control over color creation, you'll find more details on the Custom Color Selection window in the Windows user's guide that comes with Windows.)

## Saving and Removing Color Schemes

Once you create a custom color scheme, you can add it to the Color Schemes list by clicking the Save Scheme button. A small dialog box opens, where you can type in a scheme name and then click the OK button. Your color scheme then appears in the Color Schemes list, where you can choose it later.

If you're really sick of a color scheme and don't want to see it listed, get rid of it by first selecting it in the Color Schemes list, then clicking the Remove Scheme button. If you answer *Yes* when Windows asks you to confirm, the color scheme is erased from disk, and you won't see it in the Color Schemes list anymore.

# Customizing Your Desktop

The desktop that lurks behind the windows and icons on your monitor is usually a drab color. You can change the color with the Color option, but if you really want to give it pizzazz, use the Desktop window, shown in Figure 9-5, to add texture to the background or to lay down a picture on the desktop. You can also use the Desktop window to set the way windows and icons are spaced on the desktop, to change the speed at which a text cursor blinks, and to control other similar desktop quirks.

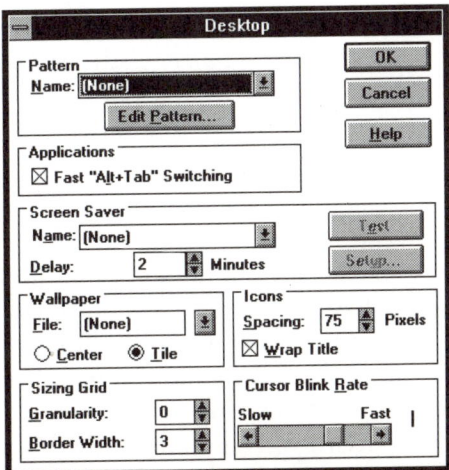

*Figure 9-5* The Desktop window offers controls that change the appearance and operation of your desktop.

## Changing the Desktop Appearance

A simple way to change the desktop appearance is by adding a pattern of black to the background color by choosing a name from the Pattern list box at the top of the Desktop window. Click *OK* to close the Desktop window, and the pattern appears on the desktop as shown in Figure 9-6. Because the pattern is black, it's best to set a light desktop color in the Colors window. If you use darker colors, you may not be able to see the pattern.

*Figure 9-6* A pattern (Waffle, in this case) is superimposed in black on the desktop.

To turn patterns off, choose *(None)* in the Pattern list box. To create your own patterns (if you have an artistic flair), click on the Edit Pattern button, which opens a small pattern editing window shown in Figure 9-7. You can click in the central box to turn dots in the pattern on and off, and you can see the results in the Sample box to its left. If you like the pattern when you're finished, save it by entering a new name and clicking *Add*. Click *OK* to exit the window and use your new pattern.

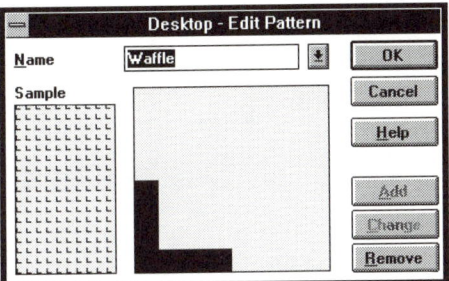

*Figure 9-7* Create your own pattern in the pattern editing window.

For a really colorful desktop, use *wallpaper,* a feature that lays a picture down on the desktop. The Wallpaper section of the Desktop window includes a list box that shows all the .bmp files (the kind that you save from Paintbrush) that are stored in Windows' home directory. When you choose a file from the list box, Windows puts its picture on the desktop, using one of two methods: centering it, in which case you see a single copy of the picture in the center of the screen, with the desktop background surrounding it; or tiling it, in which case the picture is copied in columns and rows, filling the entire desktop like tiles. You choose centering or tiling by clicking either *Center* or *Tile* in the Wallpaper area after you select a wallpaper picture.

Because most of the standard wallpaper files included with Windows are very small, centering isn't very effective. You'll only see a small picture in the center of the screen, which is easily covered by a single window on the desktop. Use tiling instead for these files.

Try using wallpaper now:

1. Double-click the Desktop icon in Control Panel to open the Desktop window.

2. Choose the file *leaves.bmp* from the Wallpaper File list box.

3. Click on the Tile button if it isn't already selected.

4. Click *OK* to close the Desktop window.

   Leaves appear on your desktop, and all icons and open windows appear on top of the leaves.

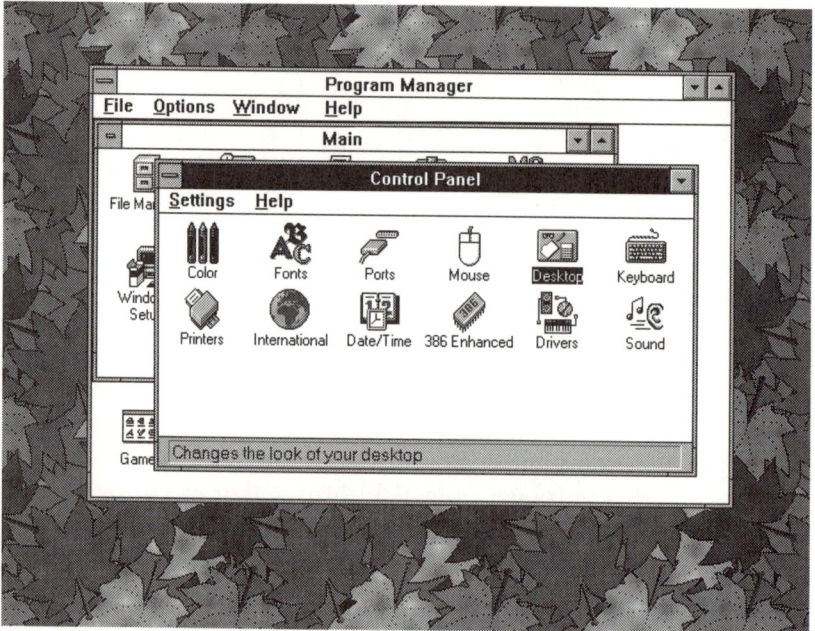

Note that whenever you use a wallpaper desktop, the wallpaper covers up any color or pattern you set for the desktop, unless the desktop background appears around the edge of centered wallpaper. Note also that although windows and icons always appear on top of the wallpaper, a busy wallpaper can make it difficult to see icon labels or icons themselves, so choose wisely.

If you're artistic and feel like creating your own wallpaper, you can use Paintbrush to draw a pattern and then save it as a file in Windows' home directory (usually c:\windows or c:\win386). You can then select the file as wallpaper in Desktop, and either tile it if it's small, or center it if it's big.

## Setting a Screen Saver

It's an unpleasant fact that any video tube that displays the same image for a long period of time can "burn in" the image so that it remains there, ghostlike, for the life of the tube. If you leave your computer running unattended for a long period of time, you may burn in an image of an open window. To prevent that, Windows provides a set of *screen savers*.

A screen saver is a small program that watches for an inactive computer. If it doesn't detect any keystrokes or mouse movements for a set period of time, it either blanks the screen or draws something that constantly changes on the screen to prevent burn-in. As soon as you type something or roll the mouse, the screen saver restores the screen as it was when you left, so you can resume working.

To set a screen saver, choose one from the Screen Saver Name list box in the Desktop window. Once chosen, you can see how it works by clicking the Test button next to the list box. To stop the test, simply roll the mouse or press a key on the keyboard. To set the amount of time a screen saver waits on an unattended computer before it starts up, enter a number of minutes in the Delay box in the Screen Saver area. The standard delay time is two minutes.

Try turning on a screen saver now:

1. Double-click the Desktop icon in Control Panel to open the Desktop window.

2. Choose *Starfield Simulation* in the Screen Saver Name list.

3. Click *Test*.

   The screen turns black, and you see stars streaming out of the center of the screen.

4. Roll the mouse.

   The screen returns to normal, and the test ends.

5. Click *OK* to close the Desktop window and put the screen saver in effect.

6. Wait for two minutes without touching your keyboard or mouse.

   The starfield appears.

7. Roll your mouse or press a key to stop the screen saver.

You now have a screen saver turned on to help protect your monitor screen. If you don't like the way it works, you can alter some of its characteristics by returning to the Desktop window, where you can click the Setup button in the Screen Saver area. It opens a setup window for the current screen saver, where you can control the number of elements it draws, its speed, and other characteristics that depend on the screen saver.

One of the options available for screen savers in the Setup Window is a password, which you can set by turning on the Password Protected check box, clicking *Set Password* to open the Change Password dialog box, and then entering a password. (You'll find details in the Windows user's guide.) Once you set a password, you'll have to enter that password to return to your normal screen, whenever the screen saver starts. This protects your unattended computer from unauthorized fiddling, but you'd better make sure that you don't forget the password!

## Miscellaneous Desktop Controls

You'll find other controls in the Desktop window that set minor characteristics of the desktop. Chances are you won't use them often, but in case you do, here they are.

### The Applications Area

The Applications area turns fast application switching on and off. When the check box is on, you can press Alt+Tab repeatedly to see the names of currently running programs and jump to the displayed program when you release the keys (as described in Chapter 6). When the check box is turned off, pressing Alt+Tab switches from program to program on each press, instead of showing you the program names. It's much slower, so there's no real reason to turn this option off.

### The Icons Area

The Icons area controls the spacing and labeling of application icons (but not document icons within application windows). The value you enter in the Spacing box controls the spacing set between icons when you arrange them with Task List or the Program Manager menu. 75 pixels (a pixel is a single dot of color on your screen) is the normal setting; set it higher for more space between icons, lower for less space between icons.

The Wrap Title check box controls icon labeling. If you turn off Wrap Title, Windows puts all icon titles in a single line of text below each icon, which often leads to overlapping (and confusing) icon titles. If you turn Wrap Title on, Windows breaks long icon titles into two or more lines, so titles don't overlap horizontally.

### The Cursor Blink Rate Area

The slider in the Cursor Blink Rate area controls how quickly the text cursor blinks in a window. The cursor blinks to attract your attention so you can find the cursor in a large area of text. If the blink is too distracting, drag the slider left to slow it down. If you have trouble finding the cursor, drag the slider right to speed the blink up.

### The Sizing Grid Area

The Sizing Grid area controls the placement of windows on the desktop and the width of window borders. The value in Granularity controls window position. If you set the value to one or more, a window "snaps" whenever you drag it, adhering to an invisible grid that forces windows to lie on the desktop with regular spacing. The higher the number, the larger the grid and the further the spacing. If the number is zero, the grid is turned off, and you can drag a window to any position on the desktop—which is usually the setting you want.

The value in the Border Width box sets the width in pixels of window borders. This is normally three, but you can set it to be as skinny as one pixel or as fat as 50 pixels. A border less than three pixels wide is a little hard to grab and drag, so test it first. And fat borders take up a lot of screen space—but you sure won't miss seeing them when you look at the window!

# Controlling Windows' Response to You

You use the mouse and keyboard to work with Windows, and the way they perform has quite a bit to do with the feel of Windows' response to your actions. If you don't like that feel, you can change it in the Mouse and Keyboard windows.

## Setting Mouse Response

To set mouse response, open the Mouse window shown in Figure 9-8. The Mouse Tracking Speed slider controls rolling. If you set it to a faster speed, the pointer moves further for a roll of the mouse than it did before. This means that small hand motions result in large pointer distances, useful if you have a steady hand and only a small amount of mouse space next to your computer. If you set the slider to a slower setting, the pointer moves a smaller distance for a roll of the mouse, convenient if you have plenty of mouse space or if you find it hard to position the pointer exactly where you want it on the desktop.

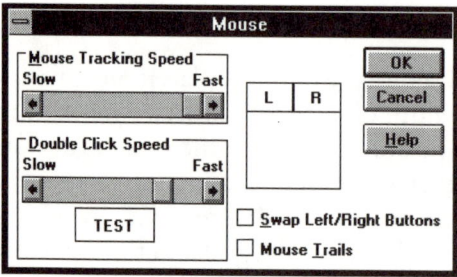

*Figure 9-8* The controls in the Mouse window set the way the mouse responds to you.

The Double Click Speed slider controls the amount of time necessary between mouse button clicks to make your clicks an official double click. A faster setting means that you must click twice very quickly to double-click; a slower setting means that you can click twice slowly to double-click. Beware of a setting that's too fast—you might find it hard to double-click quickly enough. Likewise, beware of a setting that's too slow—you might find that you're opening icons with a double click, when you thought you were making two single clicks.

If you're left handed, you'll appreciate the Swap Left/Right Buttons setting which, when turned on, swaps the function of the two mouse buttons. This means that if you roll the mouse with your left hand, you can click with your index finger (the right button) instead of your second finger (the left button). You can also use this setting to confuse right-handed friends.

The last option, Mouse Trails, helps you see the pointer on a slow-displaying LCD screen that doesn't display a quick-moving pointer well. When you turn the option on, Windows adds a trail of after-images to your pointer, which helps the pointer show up on the LCD screen. If you turn this option on with a normal screen, you might feel as if you're having eye problems.

Note that if you don't use a mouse, or if you use a non-Microsoft mouse, you may not have the same Mouse option available in Control Panel. You should have a different option that works with your pointing device; you'll have to check the instructions that came with it to see how it works.

## Setting Keyboard Response

To set keyboard response, open the Keyboard window shown in Figure 9-9. Two sliders here control the way your keyboard repeats a character when you hold down a key—a very handy feature for typing in rows of characters, such as dashes or underlines.

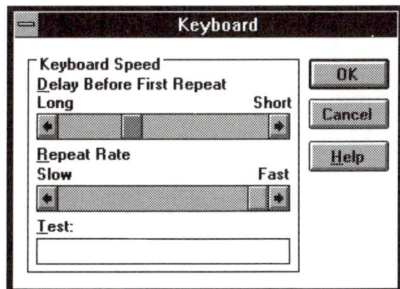

*Figure 9-9* The Keyboard window controls the response of your keyboard.

The Delay Before First Repeat slider controls the amount of time the keyboard waits when you hold down a key before it starts repeating the character. If you find that you get accidentally repeated characters while typing, then you should move the slider in the *Long* direction to increase the waiting time. If you feel like you have to hold a key forever to get repeated characters, move the slider in the *Short* direction.

The Repeat Rate controls the speed at which the keyboard puts repeated characters on the screen. Use a faster setting if you like to see characters zip out at machine gun speed; use a slower setting if you want a more leisurely pace that you can more easily control.

## Setting Date and Time

Most computers have a built-in clock, run on batteries, that keeps the current date and time even when your computer is switched off. This clock is responsible for assigning the date and time when you create or modify a file, and for adding automatic time and date to documents created in some applications. Like most clocks, the computer's clock can occasionally gain or lose time and might have to be changed at times for Daylight Savings Time. If you need to reset the time or date, open the Date & Time window shown in Figure 9-10.

*Figure 9-10* Reset the date or the time in the Date & Time window.

To reset any of the values in either the Date or Time area, select the value you want (it might be the month, minutes, AM/PM, or other value) by dragging over it with the pointer. You can then type in a new value, or you can click on the up or down arrow to the side of the area to increase or decrease the value. For example, to move the time ahead by one hour, you select the first two numerals in the Time area and then click the up arrow. Once you have the date and time set correctly, click *OK* to close the Date & Time window.

## Controlling Sound

Although you probably don't think about it, Windows often communicates with you through sound—usually a beep to tell you that what you're trying to do won't work. If you're annoyed by the beep, you can shut it off. And if you have a computer with a correctly installed sound card, you can replace the beep with a much more appealing (or at least much more complex) sound, using the Sound window shown in Figure 9-11.

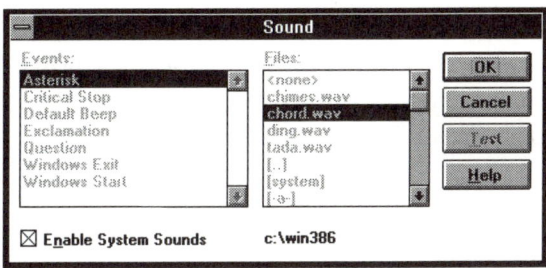

*Figure 9-11*  Use the Sound window to turn off beeps or to assign unique sounds to different Windows events.

To turn off the beep, open the Sound window, turn off the Enable System Sounds check box, and click *OK* to close the window. Windows will be perfectly silent while you work with it, except for the beep when you start Windows and the beep when you quit Windows. Turn the check box back on if you'd like to hear the beeps again.

If you have a sound card and want to make some fancy noises, you can assign different sounds to different types of Windows events, which are listed in the Events list of the Sound window. These events are, unfortunately, ambiguously named and used: different applications use different events in different ways. For example, one application may use the Asterisk sound to signify a message opening, while another application uses the Exclamation sound for the same purpose. You'll have to experiment to find out which applications use which events. Two events are standard: Windows Start, which sets the sound made when you start Windows; and Windows Exit, which sets the sound made when you quit Windows.

To assign a sound to an event, click the event in the Events list to select it, then click a sound file in the Files list to assign that file to the event. Each sound in the Files list is a waveform file ending with .wav, which is a digital recording of a sound. Whenever a specific event occurs in Windows, the sound associated with it plays. If you want to turn off the sound for a specific event (for example, you don't want a Windows Start or Windows Exit sound), you can assign *<none>* to the event.

## Other Options for Customizing Windows

Although this book can't cover all the options available in Control Panel, you can play with them if you'd like, using online help to explain controls. You'll find:

- **Fonts**  Lets you add more fonts to use in your text applications
- **Ports**  Controls the data transmission to hardware attached to your computer's ports
- **Printer**  Sets up a connected printer to work with your computer (explained in Appendix A)
- **International**  Sets keyboard layout, date, number formats, and other standards to match those used in countries around the world.

You may also find:

- **Network**  Controls your connection to a computer network
- **386 Enhanced**  Optimizes the way your 386 computer runs Windows
- **Drivers**  Installs additional devices, such as sound cards, on your computer
- **MIDI Mapper**  Controls synthesizers that are attached to your computer

And with the end of this chapter, you come not only to the end of this section, but to the end of this book. You can now rightfully claim to be introduced to Windows. May you have a long and fruitful relationship!

# APPENDIX

# A

---

# INSTALLING WINDOWS

If your computer does not yet run Windows 3.1, you must install Windows using the floppy disks that come in the Windows package. Microsoft has done an admirable job of making installation simple: You run a setup program that checks your computer system to see what kind of hardware and software it uses. It then installs Windows in the correct configuration to use that hardware and software. Along the way you answer a few simple questions, but for the most part you sit back and let the setup program do the work.

This appendix shows you a typical Windows installation. It doesn't cover every possible contingency—impossible, given the number of different computer types and accessories in the world—but it does show you how Windows is installed on a standard IBM-compatible system with a single printer attached. It also gives you instructions for adding a new printer to your system once you've already installed Windows.

## Computer System Requirements

To install and run Windows on your computer, your computer must have at least:

- An 80286 processor (Early models, such as the original IBM PC, won't run Windows because their processor isn't powerful enough.)
- 640 kilobytes of conventional memory
- 256 kilobytes of extended memory
- A hard disk drive with at least six megabytes of free space
- A floppy disk drive
- A monitor driven by an appropriate display adapter (typically EGA, VGA, Super VGA, Video 7, XGA, or similar graphics display)
- MS-DOS version 3.1 (or later) running on it

To run Windows at its best, you should consider using a computer with more powerful features:

- An 80386 or faster processor
- One or more megabytes of extended memory
- A hard disk drive with more than eight megabytes of free space

Some accessories aren't absolutely necessary, but they are highly recommended:

- A mouse or similar pointing device to quickly and easily use Windows' features
- A printer to print documents from Windows applications
- A modem to use Windows communications applications

## Installation Overview

When you install Windows 3.1 on your computer, you run a program named Setup from a floppy disk. Setup checks your computer system to see what kind of hardware you have installed (processor, memory, display adaptor, keyboard, and other standard equipment) and looks to see if you already have Windows version 3.0 installed on your hard disk drive. If you do, Setup updates that version of Windows—that is, replaces it with Windows 3.1, which is the most recent and powerful version. Setup saves as much of your previous Windows work environment as possible (program groups in Program Manager and so forth) and replaces only the files necessary for upgrading.

If you've never installed any version of Windows on your computer, Setup installs all Windows files from scratch, and sets up a *default* working environment—that is, the standard working environment as it appears before you or any other Windows users alter it for comfort. The chapters of this book describe Windows as it appears with the default working environment.

Setup can install (or update) Windows in two different ways: *express installation,* which is almost completely automated, or *custom installation,* where you have to tell Setup what to do for almost every step of the way. Although custom installation is useful for advanced users who want to fine-tune the way Windows is configured for their computer system, as a beginning user you should use express installation, which allows Setup to install the Windows configuration it thinks will best match your computer system. In most cases, it's absolutely right.

Once installation begins, Setup copies files from the Windows floppy disk set onto your hard disk. When it's finished, it queries you about your printer: what kind do you have, and where is it attached to your computer? It may also ask you questions about program files you may already have on your hard disk. When it's finished, Setup quits and (at your choice) either returns you to MS-DOS, where you started, or completely restarts your computer so that all the settings it made can take effect.

## The Installation Procedure

To run Setup and install Windows 3.1 on your computer, you need the Windows floppy disk set. You also need to know what kind of printer you have (if any) and where it's attached—normally at LPT1, the standard printer port on the back of your computer.

As you go through Windows installation, keep in mind some simple rules of thumb:

- When in doubt, press Enter. Whenever Setup presents you with a list of options, it always proposes one that it thinks is best. When you press Enter, you choose that option.

- Press Tab to move from area to area in a Setup window (for example, from text box to text box). Use the up and down arrow keys to move up and down through a list of options. Press Enter when you have set the options the way you like them.

- If all else fails, press F3. F3 stops Windows installation completely. Use this only if everything seems to be going terribly wrong (which it shouldn't).

Follow these steps to start installation:

1. Turn on your computer and wait for the MS-DOS prompt, which should be C> (or perhaps D> or E>, if your computer is set up a little differently).

2. Insert Disk #1 of the Windows floppy disk set into the floppy disk drive.

3. Change to the floppy drive: Type a: and press Enter. (If your disk is in drive B, you must type b: instead.)

4. Type setup and press Enter.

   Setup starts and displays messages that tell you it's checking the currently running software and looking for previous versions of Windows. It then asks if you want to use express or custom installation.

5. Press Enter to choose express installation.

When Setup starts to install Windows, it copies files from the floppy disk set. It prompts you whenever it's finished with one disk and needs another, at which point you should eject the floppy disk in the drive, insert the requested disk, and press Enter.

At a point about one third of the way through installation, Setup will have copied enough files to the hard disk to start Windows, so it does, and Windows appears on your monitor screen. Setup continues running as a Windows program. The first thing it does is to ask you for your name and company, which you can type in (press Tab to move from box to box and Enter when you're finished). Setup then copies more files from floppy disk to hard disk. Continue inserting new disks at its prompts.

After Setup is finished copying files to your hard disk, it installs a printer driver for your printer. It presents you with a list of printer names through which you can scroll (use the up and down arrow keys) until you find and highlight the name of your printer. (If your printer isn't listed, you can select *Generic*. Tell it that you have no printer, if you have none.) Press Enter when you've chosen. Setup then presents you with a list of ports where your printer might be attached. Find and highlight the appropriate port and press Enter.

Setup continues installation by checking your hard disk for any files that might be program files. It then sets them up so you can start them easily from within Windows. If Setup isn't sure of the program's name, it may ask you to choose from several possible names. And if Setup encounters conflicting PIFs for a program (a PIF is a file accompanying a program file that tells Windows how that program is to be run), it may ask you to resolve the conflict. Just press Enter—Setup creates a new PIF and saves the old PIF, in case you or a serviceperson needs to recover it.

Windows finishes installation by offering to restart your computer or return to MS-DOS. You should restart the computer so that all of Setup's installation can take effect: eject the last floppy disk and press Enter. Once your computer has restarted, you can start Windows and try it out. You'll find instructions in Chapter 2.

# Installing a New Printer

If you connect a new printer to your computer system and you've already installed Windows, you can easily install a printer driver for the printer without reinstalling Windows. Follow these general instructions:

1. Start your computer and run Windows.
2. Start Control Panel from the Main program group of Program Manager.
3. Open the Printers option in Control Panel.
4. Click the Add button to see a list of available printer drivers.
5. Scroll through the list until you see the name of your printer, select it, then click the Install button.

   Windows prompts you to insert a floppy disk from the Windows installation set.
6. Insert the appropriate disk and click *Install*.

   Windows copies the driver to the hard disk and, when finished, includes the name of the newly added printer on the Installed Printers list.

To set the appropriate port for your new printer, follow these steps:

1. Select the printer name in the Installed Printers list.
2. Click *Connect* to see a list of possible ports.
3. Click on the name of the port to which you've connected the printer.
4. Click *OK* to accept the port and close the list.

You can add as many printers as you care to. If you add a printer which has no standard Windows driver but that comes with a Windows driver of its own, you can follow the same procedure. Just choose *Install Unlisted or Updated Printer* as the printer's name. Windows then asks you to insert the printer's own disk instead of a disk from the Windows set.

When you're finished, close the Printer dialog box and the Control Panel—you're set to print, and you'll find details in Chapter 8.

# APPENDIX
# B

---

# COMMON WINDOWS
# TASKS

This appendix lists the most common tasks you might perform in Windows, and shows you how to accomplish them using a mouse and cursor or using the keyboard alone. The list isn't exhaustive, and neither are the methods for accomplishing the tasks; the methods listed are the most direct or the most easily understood. To find tasks not listed here, consult the index.

## Working on the Desktop

| Activity | With Mouse and Cursor | With Keyboard Alone |
|---|---|---|
| To start Windows | Not possible | 1. Turn on your computer and wait for the MS-DOS prompt.<br>2. Type win and press Enter. |
| To quit Windows | Double-click the control-menu box in the upper left corner of the Program Manager window. | Press Alt+F4, then Enter. |
| To select a window or icon on the desktop | Click the window or icon. | Press Alt+Esc until the window or icon is highlighted. |
| To select a window or icon within another window | Click the window or icon. | Press Ctrl+Tab or Ctrl+F6 until the window or icon is highlighted. |
| To open the control menu of a window or icon on the desktop | Click the control-menu box in the upper left corner of the window or click the icon. | 1. Select the window or icon.<br>2. Press Alt+Spacebar |
| To open the control menu of an application window (a window within a window) | Click the control-menu box in the upper left corner of the window. | 1. Press Alt to highlight a menu name.<br>2. Press the left arrow key until the window's control menu box is highlighted and press Enter. |
| To choose a menu item | Click the menu item | Press the up or down arrow key until the menu item is highlighted and press Enter. |
| To close a menu without choosing | Click anywhere outside the menu. | Press Esc. |

*(continued)*

## Working on the Desktop  (continued)

| Activity | With Mouse and Cursor | With Keyboard Alone |
|---|---|---|
| To move a window or icon | Drag a window by its title bar (the strip on top with the window's name) and drop the window in a new location. Drag the icon by any part of its image. | 1. Choose *Move* from the window or icon's control menu. 2. Use the arrow keys to move the window's outline or the icon to a new location and press Enter. |
| To resize a window | Drag the edge of a window to stretch or shrink the window by one side, *or* | 1. Choose *Size* from the window's control menu. 2. Press an arrow key pointing to the side you want to move for sizing. |
| | Drag the corner of a window to stretch or shrink the window by two sides. | 3. Press arrow keys to move the side in or out to the size you want and press Enter. |
| To minimize a window to an icon | Click the minimize button (the down arrow in the upper right corner of the window). | Choose *Minimize* from the window's control menu. |
| To restore a window from an icon | Double-click the icon. | Select the icon and press Enter. |
| To maximize a window to full-screen size | Click the maximize button (the up arrow in the upper right corner of the window). | Choose *Maximize* from the window's control menu. |
| To restore a window from full-screen size | Click the maximize button (the dual up-down arrow in the upper right corner of the window). | Choose *Restore* from the window's control menu. |

*(continued)*

## Working on the Desktop *(continued)*

| Activity | With Mouse and Cursor | With Keyboard Alone |
|---|---|---|
| To bring a window to the top of other windows | Click the window. | 1. Hold down the Alt key.<br>2. Press Tab until the window's name appears and release the Alt key. |
| To scroll a window's workspace | Click on the scroll bar's up or down arrow to scroll a line, *or*<br><br>Click above or below the scroll box to scroll a page, *or*<br><br>Drag the scroll box up or down to scroll long distances. | 1. Select an item in the scrollable workspace.<br>2. Use the arrow keys to move item selection up, down, left, or right, *or*<br><br>Press PgUp or PgDn, or Ctrl+PgUp or Ctrl+PgDn (for left or right) |
| To close (quit) a window | Double-click the window's control-menu box. | Choose *Close* from the window's control menu. |
| To arrange application icons on the desktop | 1. Double-click the desktop to open the Task List window.<br>2. Click the Arrange Icons button. | 1. Choose *Switch To* from any window's control menu to open the Task List window.<br>2. Press Alt+A to select the Arrange Icons button. |

## Working within a Windows Application

| Activity | With Mouse and Cursor | With Keyboard Alone |
|---|---|---|
| To open a menu | Click the menu's name in the menu bar. | 1. Press Alt to highlight a name in the menu bar.<br>2. Press the left or right arrow key until the menu name you want is highlighted and press Enter. |
| To close a menu without choosing | Click anywhere outside the menu. | Press Esc. |
| To move to an area or button in a dialog box | Not necessary | Press Tab until an item in the area is selected (or press Shift+Tab to move in the opposite direction). |
| To select a command button | Click the command button. | Press the underlined letter in the command button, *or*<br><br>Press Tab until the button label is outlined, then press Enter. |
| To select an item in a list box | 1. Scroll through the list if necessary until you see the item you want.<br>2. Click the item. | 1. Move to the list box with Tab.<br>2. Press the up or down arrow keys until you highlight the item. |
| To open a drop-down list box and select an item | 1. Click the box to open it.<br>2. Click the item you want. | 1. Move to the list box with Tab.<br>2. Press the down arrow key to open it.<br>3. Move to the item you want with the up or down arrow keys.<br>4. Press Alt+Up Arrow or Alt+Down Arrow to select the item. |

*(continued)*

*Working within a Windows Application*   (*continued*)

| Activity | With Mouse and Cursor | With Keyboard Alone |
|---|---|---|
| To select an option button | Click the button. | 1. Move to the button area with Tab.<br>2. Press the up or down arrow key until the option button is turned on. |
| To turn a check box on or off | Click the check box. | 1. Move to the check box with Tab.<br>2. Press Spacebar to turn it on or off. |
| To enter text in a text box | 1. Click the text box.<br>2. Type the text. | 1. Move to the text box with Tab.<br>2. Type the text. |
| To move the cursor within text | Click the location for the cursor. | Press the arrow keys. |
| To insert text | 1. Move the cursor where you want to insert.<br>2. Type the text. | 1. Move the cursor where you want to insert.<br>2. Type the text. |
| To select text | Drag from one end of the text to the other. | 1. Move the cursor to the one end of the text.<br>2. Hold down the Shift key as you move the cursor to the other end. |
| To deselect text | Click in a new location. | Hit any arrow key. |
| To delete text | Not possible | Press Backspace to delete selected text or, if no text is selected, the character to the left of the cursor. |
| To close a dialog box without changes | Click the Cancel button. | Press Esc. |

(*continued*)

## Working within a Windows Application *(continued)*

| Activity | With Mouse and Cursor | With Keyboard Alone |
|---|---|---|
| To arrange document windows within an application window | Choose *Cascade* or *Tile* from the application window's Window menu. | Choose *Cascade* or *Tile* from the application window's Window menu. |
| To arrange document icons within an application window | Choose *Arrange Icons* from the application window's Window menu. | Choose *Arrange Icons* from the application window's Window menu. |
| To get help with using an application | Choose *Contents* from the Help menu. | Choose *Contents* from the Help menu. |
| To quit an application | Double-click the control-menu box. | Choose *Close* from the control menu. |

## Working with Multiple Programs

| | | |
|---|---|---|
| To switch from one program to another | Click the window of the program you want. | 1. Hold down the Alt key.<br>2. Press Tab until the program's name appears and release the Alt key. |
| To paste an object from one program into another program | 1. Select the object in the first program.<br>2. Choose *Copy* from the Edit menu.<br>3. Move to the second program.<br>4. Put the cursor where you want the object.<br>5. Choose *Paste* from the Edit menu. | 1. Select the object in the first program.<br>2. Choose *Copy* from the Edit menu.<br>3. Move to the second program.<br>4. Put the cursor where you want the object.<br>5. Choose *Paste* from the Edit menu. |

*(continued)*

## Working with Multiple Programs  *(continued)*

| Activity | With Mouse and Cursor | With Keyboard Alone |
|---|---|---|
| To revise an embedded object | 1. Double-click the object to start the server program.<br>2. Revise the object in the server program.<br>3. Save the changes to the object and quit the server program. | 1. Select the object.<br>2. Choose *Edit <object name> Object* from the edit menu to start the server program.<br>3. Revise the object in the server program.<br>4. Save the changes to the object and quit the server program. |

## Working with Program Manager

| | | |
|---|---|---|
| To open a program group | Double-click the group icon. | Choose the program group's name from the Window menu. |
| To start a program | Double-click the program's icon. | Select the program's icon and press Enter. |
| To create a program group | 1. Choose *New* from the File menu.<br>2. Select *Program Group* and click *OK*.<br>3. Enter the group's name in the Description text field and click *OK*. | 1. Choose *New* from the File menu.<br>2. Select *Program Group* and select the OK button.<br>3. Enter the name in the Description text field and press Enter. |
| To rename a program group | 1. Select the group.<br>2. Choose *Properties* from the File menu.<br>3. Change the text in the Description text box and click *OK*. | 1. Select the group.<br>2. Choose *Properties* from the File menu.<br>3. Change the text in the Description text box and press Enter. |

*(continued)*

## Working with Program Manager  *(continued)*

| Activity | With Mouse and Cursor | With Keyboard Alone |
|---|---|---|
| To delete a program group or a program item | 1. Select the group or item.<br>2. Choose *Delete* from the File menu and confirm your deletion. | 1. Select the group or item.<br>2. Choose *Delete* from the File menu and confirm your deletion. |
| To move a program item from one program group to another | Drag the item from one program group window and drop it on another program group window or icon. | 1. Select the item in one group.<br>2. Choose *Move* from the File menu.<br>3. Enter the name of the destination program group in the To Group text box and press Enter. |
| To set a program to start when Windows starts | Move the program's icon into the StartUp program group. | Move the program's icon into the StartUp program group. |

## Working with File Manager

| Activity | With Mouse and Cursor | With Keyboard Alone |
|---|---|---|
| To view the contents of a disk or other volume | Click on the disk or volume's icon in the volume icon area (just below the menu bar). | 1. Press Tab to move to the volume icon area (just below the menu bar).<br>2. Use the left and right arrow keys to select the volume you want, then press Enter. |
| To see the full directory tree of a volume | Choose *Expand All* from the Tree menu. | Choose *Expand All* from the Tree menu. |
| To expand or contract a directory tree branch by one level | Double-click the icon at the base of the branch in the directory tree. | Select the directory icon in the directory tree area and press Enter. |

*(continued)*

## Working with File Manager *(continued)*

| Activity | With Mouse and Cursor | With Keyboard Alone |
|---|---|---|
| To view the contents of a directory | Click the directory icon in the directory tree to select the directory. Its contents appear in the directory contents area. | 1. Use Tab to move to the directory tree area.<br>2. Press the up or down arrow keys to move to the directory in the tree. Its contents appear in the directory contents area. |
| To search for a file | 1. Choose *Search* from the File menu.<br>2. Enter the file's name in the Search For text box and press Enter. | 1. Choose *Search* from the File menu.<br>2. Enter the file's name in the Search For text box and press Enter. |
| To start a program or open a document | Double-click the program or document icon in the directory contents area. | Select the program or document icon in the directory contents area and press Enter. |
| To create a new directory | 1. Select the directory in the directory tree where you want the new directory placed.<br>2. Choose *Create Directory* from the File menu.<br>3. Enter a name in the Name text box and press Enter. | 1. Select the directory in the directory tree where you want the new directory placed.<br>2. Choose *Create Directory* from the File menu.<br>3. Enter a name in the Name text box and press Enter. |
| To move a file or directory | Drag the file or directory's icon and drop it on the directory where you want it moved. | 1. Select the file or directory's icon.<br>2. Choose *Move* from the File menu.<br>3. Enter the name of the destination directory in the To text box and press Enter. |

*(continued)*

## Working with File Manager *(continued)*

| Activity | With Mouse and Cursor | With Keyboard Alone |
|---|---|---|
| To copy a file or directory | Hold down the Ctrl key, drag the file or directory's icon, and drop it on the directory where you want it copied. | 1. Select the file or directory's icon.<br>2. Choose *Copy* from the File menu.<br>3. Enter the name of the destination directory in the To text box and press Enter. |
| To rename a file or directory | 1. Select the file or directory's icon.<br>2. Choose *Rename* from the File menu.<br>3. Enter the new name in the To text box and press Enter. | 1. Select the file or directory's icon.<br>2. Choose *Rename* from the File menu.<br>3. Enter the new name in the To text box and press Enter. |
| To delete a file or directory | 1. Select the file or directory's icon.<br>2. Choose *Delete* from the File menu and answer *Yes* to all confirmation notices. (If a directory contains files, you can confirm *Yes to All* to delete all those files at once.) | 1. Select the file or directory's icon.<br>2. Choose *Delete* from the File menu and answer *Yes* to all confirmation notices. (If a directory contains files, you can confirm *Yes to All* to delete all those files at once.) |
| To format a floppy disk | 1. Insert the floppy disk in the drive where you want to format.<br>2. Choose *Format Disk* from the Drive menu.<br>3. Select the drive and the capacity at which you want to format.<br>4. Click *OK* and follow the instructions. | 1. Insert the floppy disk in the drive where you want to format.<br>2. Choose *Format Disk* from the Drive menu.<br>3. Select the drive and the capacity at which you want to format.<br>4. Select *OK* and follow the instructions. |

*(continued)*

## Working with File Manager  (continued)

| Activity | With Mouse and Cursor | With Keyboard Alone |
|---|---|---|
| To copy a floppy disk | 1. Write-protect the original disk.<br>2. Choose *Copy Disk* from the Disk menu and confirm.<br>3. Follow the instructions on screen. | 1. Write-protect the original disk.<br>2. Choose *Copy Disk* from the Disk menu and confirm.<br>3. Follow the instructions on screen. |

## Working with Print Manager

| | | |
|---|---|---|
| To pause and resume printing | Click the Pause button to pause, the Resume button to resume. | Press Alt+P to pause, Alt+R to resume. |
| To change the order of print jobs in the queue | Drag the job up or down the queue and drop it in a new location. (You can't change the position of the first job.) | 1. Select the job you want with the up or down arrow keys.<br>2. Hold down the Ctrl key and press the up or down arrow keys until the job outline appears in the position you want, then release the Ctrl key. |
| To delete a print job | 1. Select the print job.<br>2. Click the *Delete* button and confirm. | 1. Select the print job.<br>2. Press Alt+D and confirm. |

## *Working with Control Panel*

| Activity | With Mouse and Cursor | With Keyboard Alone |
|---|---|---|
| To set a color scheme | 1. Double-click the Color option.<br>2. Choose a new color scheme from the Color Scheme list box<br>3. Click the OK button. | 1. Select the Color option and press Enter.<br>2. Choose a new color scheme from the Color Scheme list box.<br>3. Select the OK button. |
| To wallpaper the desktop | 1. Double-click the Desktop option.<br>2. Choose a wallpaper pattern from the File list box in the Wallpaper area.<br>3. Choose *Tile* to repeat the wallpaper picture across the desktop, or *Center* to put a single picture in the center.<br>4. Click the OK button. | 1. Select the Desktop option and press Enter.<br>2. Choose a wallpaper pattern from the File list box in the Wallpaper area.<br>3. Choose *Tile* to repeat the wallpaper picture across the desktop, or *Center* to put a single picture in the center.<br>4. Select the OK button. |
| To turn on a screen saver | 1. Double-click the Desktop option.<br>2. Choose a screen saver from the Name list box in the Screen Saver area (or *None* to turn it off).<br>3. Click the OK button. | 1. Select the Desktop option and press Enter.<br>2. Choose a screen saver from the Name list box in the Screen Saver area (or *None* to turn it off).<br>3. Select the OK button. |
| To set mouse response: (tracking, double-click speed) | 1. Double-click the Mouse option.<br>2. Set the two sliders to control the speed of the pointer on the screen and the rate you must double-click.<br>3. Click the OK button. | 1. Select the Mouse option and press Enter.<br>2. Set the two sliders to control the speed of the pointer on the screen and the rate you must double-click.<br>3. Select the OK button. |

*(continued)*

## Working with Control Panel  *(continued)*

| Activity | With Mouse and Cursor | With Keyboard Alone |
|---|---|---|
| To set keyboard response: (delay before repeat, repeat rate) | 1. Double-click the Keyboard option. 2. Set the two sliders to control the period of time before keyboard repeat sets in and the rate of the repeat. 3. Click the OK button. | 1. Select the Keyboard option and press Enter. 2. Set the two sliders to control the period of time before keyboard repeat sets in and the rate of the repeat. 3. Select the OK button. |
| To set current date and time | 1. Double-click the Date/Time option. 2. Select any part of the date or time by dragging over it. 3. Adjust the value by clicking the up or down arrow on the same line. 4. Click the OK button. | 1. Select the Date/Time option and press Enter. 2. Select any part of the date or time by pressing Tab. 3. Adjust the value by typing in a new one and press Enter. |

# INDEX

The book you hold in your hands

embodies a new concept in computer book publishing.

The cover photo is by Scott Morgan.

The cover and title page concepts were designed by award-winning

designer Christopher Johnson, who lives and works in New York City.

The interior book design is by Carol Barth of Modern Design, in Los Angeles.

The interior text of the book was composed by Modern Design using

Aldus PageMaker 4.01 on Apple Macintosh computers.

The body text is $^{11}/_{12}$ Adobe Garamond.

The cover was designed on a Macintosh computer as well and uses

Franklin Gothic and Adobe Garamond typefaces.